THE
FUNDAMENTALS OF
INSURANCE

THE
FUNDAMENTALS OF
INSURANCE

THEORIES, PRINCIPLES AND PRACTICES

HARGOVIND DAYAL

Notion Press

Old No. 38, New No. 6
McNichols Road, Chetpet
Chennai - 600 031

First Published by Notion Press 2017
Copyright © Hargovind Dayal 2017
All Rights Reserved.

ISBN 978-1-947949-67-6

Contents

Table of Figures, Graphs and Charts

Figures

Tables

Acknowledgements

21st June, 2017.

Finally, after many days, weeks and months, I finished writing this book. From the initial 'idea' through to the stages of planning, researching, writing, revising, editing and proof reading, and the various stages of the publication process, was a very long journey. It was made possible by the invaluable inputs and goodwill of my many friends.

While serving at United India Insurance Co. Ltd., and subsequently at Reliance General Insurance Co. Ltd., my friends and colleagues helped me learn what I know about Insurance, about what 'works,' why and how. Observation also taught me something about what should not be done. I have tried to incorporate my experience in the text, but must apologise for errors, omissions and ambiguities that may have unwittingly crept into it. And, I sincerely hope that Readers will contribute suggestions that shall help me remove these aberrations and improve the text.

Throughout this book, but specially in Chapters 9 and 10 observations and analysis offered has been made on the basis of authentic data made available in the public domain by the Insurance Regulatory and Development Authority of India through its comprehensive and erudite publication the "Journal" which is published every month and its Annual Reports. Readers, if desirous, are invited to refer to these for more details and statistics.

I owe so much to so many that it would not be possible to record my gratitude for every individual. Yet I must acknowledge some special contributions. Apoorv Tatia and Kirti Kothari, my colleagues at Reliance General, provided inputs on Micro Insurance and Life Insurance, respectively. My son, Uday Dayal acted as a catalyst, and persuaded me to write this book and Preety Dayal, my spouse, patiently provided unending encouragement every time I faltered. Aloke Gupta, my friend, and colleague from my time at United India, diligently corrected and proof-read chapters 1 to 18. The team at Notion Press, headed by Naveen Valsakumar, patiently waited for me to complete the manuscript and Selvinds George, the Project Manager, my 'Go To' man and his quietly efficient team designed the covers and interiors, performed quality checks that transformed it into a book. Finally, the efforts of the 'Print' team have helped place this volume in your hands.

'Thanks' does not adequately express my gratitude to everyone who helped me along the way.

Hargovind Dayal

Agra

Email: hargovind.dayal@yahoo.co.in

An Introduction to This Book – the 'Why,' 'What' and 'How'

As with a lot else in life, 'chance' had much to do with my decision to write this book. One evening, a student enrolled in an Undergraduate Program in Management happened to ask me some questions about aspects of insurance which were part of his curriculum. I could see that he was struggling with a subject which many find less than 'exciting,' especially in the way it is presented in textbooks and classrooms. I tried to provide some answers and this led us to more questions. Gradually, but steadily, as pieces of the puzzle began to fall into place, the mundane became significant and the 'student' developed a perspective on the connection between insurance and the national economy. Somewhere along the way I realised what I wanted to do. Writing this book seemed to be the best way to share with other students and readers this structured view and understanding of how 'Insurance' connected with both their individual lives and the economic life of the nation.

Yet, though I certainly hope it will help students with their syllabi, this book is not meant to be another textbook. In fact, it is also designed as a 'Reference' Text for practicing Managers, many of who migrate to the insurance function as an additional responsibility while serving in the 'Finance' function for their Employers, in Industry, Manufacturing or even the Banking and Financial Services workspace which covers Bancassurance and Financial Product distribution.

Books on Insurance often begin with a definition and explanation of Risk, its types, and the methods of managing risk. They lead the reader straight into a set of concepts without educating him about the context in which the concepts attain their relevance.

This book takes a different route. It takes a step back, and makes the reader first look at the context and then at the concept. It uses the setting of everyday life to help the reader comprehend the constant exposure to risk for all of us in everything we do. Risk is much more pervasive, in a sense more 24/7 than Call Centers or anything we have imagined, and it impacts us in a 360° way little else does. Once a person comes to understand this basic fact, the act of buying and selling insurance will never be the routine business of making another investment, of pushing a sale, of achieving an Annual target or simply saving tax. It becomes the vital act of protection for cherished assets, an essential part of the foundation of modern industrial society and everyday life.

Throughout this book theories are explained in the context of the world around us, with examples which the reader can relate to events experienced directly or through peers. When theories get connected to reality as we experience it they ceases to be 'theoretical,' and we travel beyond knowing facts to 'understanding' them. This book is an earnest attempt at helping the reader achieve an 'understanding,' and hopefully in the end it succeeds in making Insurance understood as something much more significant than a mundane, 'dry as dust' business transaction that can be conveniently relegated to a slot towards the end of the agenda, the position which it usually occupies for most individuals or businesses.

In terms of structure, this book consists of 18 Chapters grouped into 4 Sections, each of which prepares the conceptual ground for the next.

In the end, I hope that this book shall broaden the reader's perspective of why we need insurance, what it offers as a tool for managing risk, and how the insurance ecosphere functions.

Hargovind Dayal

Agra

14th June, 2017.

SECTION I

INSURANCE AND THE ECONOMY
– A View through the Telescope

Think back to the last time you looked at some new, faraway, landscape through a telescope. In all likelihood you began by panning across the vista, then slowly began to zoom in on significant features which stood out, and finally at maximum magnification, you closely examined the landscape, perhaps concentrating on some landmark which may have been of special interest to you. In this way you came to develop both an overall perspective of the landscape and a detailed, intimate knowledge of that special feature or landmark which interested you. Finally, you came to possess an 'understanding' of what you had seen.

The first Section of this book invites you to look at Insurance through the 'telescope.' It presents insurance both from the 'macro' point of view as a cog in the national economic machine, and as it impacts the everyday lives of individuals.

Chapters 1 to 3 introduce the readers first to the 'big picture' of risk as it exists all around us, then takes them on to explain how it is managed and mitigated through systematic techniques, briefly recounting how Insurance developed historically. This is followed by an explanation of the interdependence of Commerce, Manufacturing and Banking, the crucial role of Insurance in providing the 'safety net' for Banking, and the relationship between these factors and economic development. The chapters are brief, but direct in their approach, and prepare the foundation for a discussion of the basic concepts of insurance that follows.

CHAPTER I
The Business Domain

Understanding the General Insurance Universe; the Existence of Risk and the different 'Lines of Business'; Motor Insurance; Health and Accident Insurance; Property Insurance; Marine Insurance; Liability Insurance; Insurance of Agriculture and Rural Assets

Life Insurance

It is an often repeated truism that human life is more precious than the most invaluable material asset. None will dispute this in spite of the callous disregard for human life and the inordinate care for property which we sometimes witness. Certainly, a person's life is more precious to him than all his assets, and furthermore, loss of it would also adversely affect the family members and dependants who are sustained by him. The perils and risks to which human life is exposed are extremely varied, and life insurance commenced as a device that offered 'compensation' for loss of life during a defined 'term' or period. Subsequently it morphed into an instrument for savings and 'investment' in addition to its original purpose. Eventually, by a curious perversion of logic and purpose it has even come to be sold as a tool for efficient 'tax management' rather than for the 'risk protection' for which it was originally intended. However, this is a thread which we shall take up later during this narrative. For the moment it is sufficient to observe that life insurance originated as a risk protection device that offered compensation for the loss of human life.

General Insurance

The business of 'General Insurance' is often also referred to as 'Non-Life' Insurance to distinguish it from the business of 'Life' Insurance. The objective of 'Life' Insurance policy is evident from the name itself, but you could well ask, what is the purpose of 'General Insurance,' what does it do? What sort of protection does it offer? Who is protected, against what, how, and for what value? These are important questions, but before we try to answer them, let us first try to demarcate the business domain of 'General Insurance.'

Imagine yourself seated inside a Spacecraft, flying at a very high altitude, looking down at Earth through a powerful telescope. Zooming in what would you see? Presumably, you would see Ships sailing the oceans, Airplanes flying, taking off or landing. Zooming in further you would see farms, towns and cities, tall buildings, factories, railways, trucks, cars, shops and homes, and people everywhere. Everything that you see except human life falls in the business domain of General Insurance. From Ships, Airplanes, Motor Vehicles, the Cargo being transported, Buildings and Factories, Shops and their merchandise, Hospitals to Educational Institutions, Homes and the personal possessions they contain, Farms, crops and agricultural animals, and a seemingly endless list of items is covered under the protective umbrella of General Insurance. And not just things, General Insurance policies offer protection to people for three distinct types of 'person' related contingencies. The cost of medical treatment in hospitals, compensation for permanent disabilities resulting from accidents, and legal liabilities are all covered by specific products. This is broadly speaking, an answer to the question of 'what' falls in the domain of general insurance business.

At his point someone could actually wonder whether there is a 'need' to take protection. Against what sort of contingencies is this protection required?

The Existence of Risk and the Different 'Lines of Business'

Visualize yourself standing on a street corner, watching the world go by, as the saying goes. What can happen? Where is the risk? What can go wrong? Well, actually, and luckily, most of the time nothing goes wrong, but when it does, imagine what happens.

Motor Insurance

Most of us have read of, or even witnessed, a road accident. Consider the possible consequence of a road accident. The damaged Motor Vehicle has to be repaired, and injured persons have to be taken to hospitals for treatment. Sometimes, motor vehicles are stolen, and more often than not, they are not recovered. Any of these events can lead to very substantial losses. If some other person, also called a third party, gets injured in the accident or their property is damaged, then the vehicle owner can be hauled into a Court of Law. The compensation awarded in such cases often runs into millions. A 'Motor Insurance' policy offers protection against such eventualities.

Health and Accident Insurance

When road accidents take place people often get hurt, and that leads to painful and costly treatment at hospitals. Sometimes, it gets worse, and injuries result in permanent disablement or even death. At other times, and without warning, major diseases strike seemingly healthy people. A 'Health Insurance' policy takes care of the costs of medical treatment at a hospital, and a 'Personal Accident' policy offers compensation for temporary and permanent disabilities suffered or death.

Property Insurance

Continue to look around you, and observe the many buildings, tall skyscrapers, and smaller ones. The homes, shops and factories, the enormous variety of machinery which are an integral part of modern life, all these things, big and small, each represent an extremely high economic value, and an even higher utility, to their owners. Recall the effect of Earthquakes. They happen rarely, but their effect can be devastating. Remember the incidents of 'fire' you may have heard about. 'Fire' can swiftly grow and reduce everything nearby to ashes. Riots and strikes, fortunately, don't happen often, but when they do the damage to property, and loss of life, is extensive. What is worse is that nobody can predict these occurrences. We can, and must, try to eliminate or minimize the losses, and build earthquake-resistant buildings, implement various fire safety measures, and as a 'Society' work with the 'State' to prevent the occurrence of riots and strikes. Yet, since none can guarantee that such events will never happen, prudence indicates the benefit of purchasing insurance protection through a 'Property Insurance' policy.

Marine Insurance

Now turn your attention away from the buildings to the highways and the railways. Observe the continuous lines of trucks, and the even more continuous movement of Railways, across the length and breadth of the country. They transport raw materials to factories and manufactured products to markets. Further afield, in an increasingly globalized world, cargo is transported through ships and airplanes, between locations separated by thousands of miles. This 24x7 movement of Cargo is exposed to the risk of various types of losses as it is transported. The insurance of cargo falls in the domain of 'Marine' insurance. The vessels or vehicles that transport the cargo are insured under separate insurance policies designed according to their respective special features and requirements. The trucks are insured under a Motor Insurance policy, the ships under 'Marine Hull' policies and airplanes under 'Aircraft Hull' policies.

Liability Insurance

Let us continue our exploration of the theme of 'Risk.' Consider the following separate but specific incidents. In the first, a person accidentally discharges a firearm and injures or kills a bystander. Second, the owner of a flat located on the upper floors of a multi-storey apartment leaves a water tap open by mistake and goes away on vacation. At that time the water supply was interrupted, but when it is resumed the water flows out and floods the common area outside the flat as well as the staircase. A neighbor loses his footing on the slippery surface, falls down and breaks his arm. In the third incident, a lady who purchased a 'Fairness' cream produced by a famous Cosmetics manufacturer finds that the cream causes her to suffer severe allergic reaction leading to acute ulceration of facial tissue. In the fourth incident, a person undergoing treatment in a hospital after a road accident finds that when the injuries have healed, and the bandages and plaster is taken off, the bones of his left leg have not set properly. The leg is now short by an inch and a half, and he now suffers from a permanent limp. These are the sort of items occasionally featured in the daily newspaper.

In each of these four incidents specific actions had caused harm to a member of the public, but the first is a 'criminal' act whereas the other three are not. The man who used the firearm is likely to be charged under the criminal laws for 'manslaughter' and tired accordingly. No insurance protection is available for this type of action. The other three are examples of 'civil liabilities' or 'torts,' and can be covered under different types of insurance policies

Insurance of Agriculture and Rural Assets

Many people, especially those who live in cities, think of farming and farmers as 'simple' and 'uncomplicated.' Yet, farming can be a tricky business, involving complex decisions about what crops to plant, the management of inputs like seed, fertilizer and water, harvesting and storage, and finally the marketing of the produce. Management skills and discipline in execution is required on a scale which we normally associate with a business enterprise. In reality, the farmer is a skilled, but often underrated entrepreneur. His productive assets, the equivalent of working capital, plant and machinery, and stock, are the agricultural inputs like seed, fertilizer, his cattle and crops, and he often relies on commercial 'credit' to finance his assets and operations. A bad monsoon, drought or excessive rain, a crop pestilence or livestock disease, all identifiable perils but unpredictable and unquantifiable risks, can determine the profit made or loss endured by him. The perils and risks are beyond his control, and insurance remains the only recourse to manage the outcome. In fact 'micro insurance' and the insurance of agricultural assets is emerging as the newest 'green field' for the insurance industry. This is a subject that shall be further discussed in Chapter 15, and also in Chapter 13.

Having identified the challenge posed by the pervasive presence of risk let us proceed to discuss how, if at all, it can be managed.

CHAPTER 2
Managing Risk

Risk Avoidance; Risk Reduction; Risk Retention; Insurance

Almost everyone accepts that 'risk' is ever present in our daily lives, and that we have to find some way to deal with it, an effective way to manage it so that the consequences are the least harmful. Professionals traditionally recognize four distinct techniques of Risk Management.

Figure 1: The Risk Management Matrix

Risk Avoidance

When faced with 'risk' in any real life situation, the first, and most obvious, countermeasure which comes to mind is 'Avoidance.' This literally consists of eliminating, or not doing, or exiting from, some activity or location with which the risk is positively associated. For example, the risk of incurring 'Third Party Liabilities arising out of road accidents' can be avoided by a person by not owning a motor vehicle. The risk of loss by earthquake to your residential house can be avoided by building or buying a residence only in a geographical location where earthquakes do not occur. The risk of theft of personal jewellery can be avoided by not possessing any jewellery, or by not wearing it. However, these are extreme measures, and most people will agree that avoidance is not an acceptable option except in a few, rare circumstances. Most of us buy motor vehicles because we need them, because they are a necessity. We build or buy houses wherever we have to live, and the location, depends upon so many important factors like livelihood, citizenship, socio-cultural roots, etc, and very few people would stop wearing jewellery because compared to other personal effect there is a high risk of it being stolen. We do what we have to in these situations, or rather, we opt for what appears to be the best possible combination of solutions for various requirements, but we do try to minimize the risks we have to face due to our choices.

Risk Reduction

No one can 'play it safe' totally all the time, and simply avoid 'risk' in everyday life. Therefore, many people develop 'safe' habits, or adopt specific procedures, explore alternatives and options which would reduce that risk. For example, someone who buys a motor vehicle also learns the various 'dos and don'ts' of safe driving, ensure that they park the vehicle in a safe place and keep it locked. They may also install a 'anti-theft' device such as an alarm, and they may resolve to they never 'drink and drive.' People considering the purchase of a house may not be able to avoid the risk of 'earthquakes' by relocating their place of residence, but they try to reduce it by opting for dwellings built with earthquake resistant techniques and materials. A person who wishes to reduce the risk of ill-health, or, let us say of suffering a 'heart attack,' can follow the general rules of good health such as not smoking, eating a balanced nutritious diet, doing physical exercise regularly, and so on, to stay healthy and fit. Factories try to reduce the risk of loss due to 'fire' by meticulously following better processes, better housekeeping, and maintaining high standards of hygiene and discipline on the shop floor. Yet, all the best techniques of risk reduction only 'reduce' the risks, they cannot eliminate it. In spite of strict adherence to the rules of safe driving, road accidents, can and will happen. Earthquake resistant buildings may be able to withstand their impact better, but the occurrence of damage cannot be ruled out, or its' extent predicted. In the most well maintained industrial establishments, incidents of 'fire' may be rare, but they do occur, and theft, whether of motor vehicles or of jewelery, cannot be totally prevented. A certain degree of risk remains after the best precautions have been taken. What is the next step?

Risk Retention or 'Self Insurance,' and Transfer of Risk

After application of risk reduction techniques it is possible that the residual risk may appear to be small enough not to worry about. A person may feel 'we can live with it.' For example, a factory manufacturing computers or garments, may reduce the risk of 'Burglary' by adopting stock handling procedures, and by building a fence around its perimeter, posting security guards 'round-the-clock' and installing CCTV cameras. At this point the Factory's Management may conclude that the risk of burglars breaking into the premises has been reduced so much that insurance protection is not required. After all, who would want to take the risk of breaking into such a well guarded premises, and that too for items which are bulky to handle or not very high in unit value. The Management may therefore decide not to take any insurance. By not taking insurance the Management of the factory has 'retained' the risk of burglary. Such acts of 'Risk Retention' are also referred to a 'Self Insurance.' We may therefore define Risk Retention as management of risk by an individual or organization, by taking upon themselves the full responsibility for all financial and legal consequences arising from the occurrence of the event which represents the risk. To effectively implement retention of risk, it would be prudent to create a 'sinking fund' or pool sufficiently large to take care of all the financial liabilities that would arise from the occurrence of risk, and to make regular contributions to the fund.

'Risk Retention' takes place in three different types of circumstances. Firstly, it can happen either when the risk is perceived to be small enough to be borne by the individual themselves. The case mentioned above is an example of this type of circumstance. Secondly, retention may also ensue when the cost of risk transfer is too high and not worth the benefit. Thirdly, retention of risk also takes place when the risk itself is such that it is considered 'uninsurable,' either because it is too large or big for an insurance company to bear it, or because it does not fit in with the purposes or objectives of insurance. However, someone who finds a risk too 'big' to bear on their own may wish to share the burden with others. They would then try to transfer all, or part of the risk to others willing to bear it. This transfer of risk, from an individual to a group, by sharing it among many, is called 'Insurance.' We can therefore view Insurance as a structured commercial activity, conducted by an Insurance Company, for the purpose of sharing of risks among a large group of people.

Insurance

Wikipedia's article on Insurance describes it in the following words:

> *"Insurance is the equitable transfer of the risk of a loss, from one entity to another in exchange for payment. It is a form of risk management primarily used to hedge against the risk of a contingent, uncertain loss."*[1]

While discussing risk retention and transfer we too had reached a similar understanding of the concept of insurance, to which Wikipedia's formulation of the idea has explicitly added the elements of 'Equitable transfer' and 'payment.' When an entity proposes to transfer its risk to another, obviously this must be done equitably. The risk transferred by one entity must be accompanied by a 'sufficient' payment to the entity which accepts the risk. In return, when a loss occurs, the latter entity must offer 'adequate' compensation to the former, who has suffered the loss. The idea of adequate compensation lies at the heart of insurance as an activity and an idea. The risk of individuals is shared among the group, and in turn the losses suffered by individual members are shared by the group in such a manner that every individual is compensated fully for the damage suffered. No person should, in the end, be left in a situation of net loss. Everyone must be restored to the same financial position in which they were placed before the loss occurred. Ideologically, you will note that insurance has a 'noble' objective, the maintenance of financial stability for society as a whole, for each individual who otherwise would be left in the lurch, often to fend for himself.

The entire activity of the transfer of risk is conducted in a highly structured manner based on the general laws of contracts to which are added some special features due to the unique nature of the insurance business. The principles of 'equity' and 'transparency' are vital elements of the transactions and the mechanism through which they are to be conducted. We will examine the basic concepts and principles of insurance in greater detail a little later. For the moment let us try to understand the strategic significance of 'insurance' to the 'economy' as a whole, especially, its relationship to other business activities such as manufacturing, finance and banking.

CHAPTER 3
Insurance in the Economic Universe

Historical role; the Business Equation Today

Historical Role

Till the middle of the 20th century the world's economies were largely 'cash dependant' and not 'credit driven.' Economic historians can quarrel about the specific date or event which marks a turning point from when 'Credit,' and not 'Cash' became the more dominant driver of economic growth, but for our general purpose it is not very material on what specific date or event they final agree upon. For a long duration of human history it was 'Cash' which was considered 'King,' the important fuel that drove the economy and commerce. Remember the old exhortation "Neither a Borrower nor a Lender be." It used to be popular with the generation of our Grandparents, or their parents, people who grew up with the mindset of the 19th century. In simple terms, people of good social standing, who belonged to the 'middle classes' or better, considered it undignified, almost less than 'moral' to borrow money. A 'debtor' fell from grace, and grew small in stature, somehow. It is not as if 'Credit' as a source of finance did not exist, but rather, its role was comparatively minor in driving economic activity. In this scenario the 'rich' who held a major portion of the 'wealth' did not need 'credit, and did not like the idea of 'borrowing' anyway. The rest, the 'poor' who could have utilized 'credit' had no access to it for the Banks would not lend them money. The Banks themselves were viewed as 'repositories' of cash rather than as 'sources' of finance. The world's economy, and commerce, continued to grow at a slow, steady, conservative pace.

Then, from the 18th century onwards, the Industrial Revolution which started in Great Britain and Europe, and spread through the world, set in motion two centuries of continuous economic expansion, which has culminated in our present state of a globalized, connected, interdependent economy. Greater exploitation of natural resources, increased supply of raw materials, an explosion of inventions and technology, all led to a massive growth in industrial output. The need to implement the new ideas and inventions created an expanding demand for finance.

Entrepreneurs and Industrialists needed 'money,' but the Banks who possessed the resources would provide access to them only if they were assured that they would be able to recover their money even if the assets financed by them were destroyed by natural calamities or accidents. The Insurance industry provided this vital assurance of protection through its policies of insurance, and therefore, as the economy expanded, the Banking system grew, and so did 'insurance.' Remember we are only saying that from this time the Insurance Industry 'grew,' and not that this is when it was started or invented. Historians have found evidence of the existence of practices of distribution of risk akin to insurance among Chinese and Babylonian traders as long ago as the 2nd and 3rd millennium BCE. The Code of Hammurabi, c.1750 BCE, records the practice of marine insurance among merchants sailing the Mediterranean Sea. In the 1680s Edward Lloyd's famous Coffee House in London became the location for a thriving marine insurance business transacted between merchants and underwriters who were its regular patrons. A few years earlier London's first 'Fire Insurance' company had started business operations. The first Life Insurance policies were perhaps taken out in America in 1706. So, there is enough evidence to establish the existence of insurance as a risk management activity long before the events of the Industrial Revolution turbocharged its growth.

The Business Equation Today

What is the equation between Insurance, Banking and the Economy? What is the relationship between Insurance and Banking, and what is the strategic role 'Insurance' plays in economic activity?

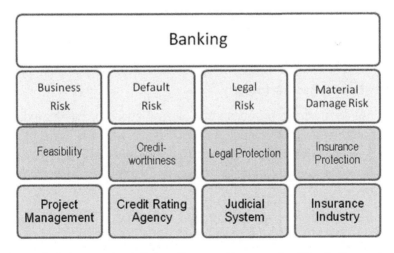

Figure 2: Insurance and Other Support Systems for Credit Expansion

Entrepreneurs, Industrialists and Traders, all need easy access to large amounts of capital to be able to grow at the rate that is now considered necessary. Without this access to capital they would have to rely solely on their own resources which would severely limit the scale and scope of their operations. Economic activity would not come to a halt, but it would slow down to a snail's pace.

A Bank's decision to provide finance for a venture, whether a new project, an industrial expansion or a commercial transaction generally depends upon four factors:

- **Business Risks – Feasibility** – as assessment of the technical and commercial feasibility of the proposed venture. *Domain Specialists in the field of Project Management & Implementation provide this input.*

- **Default Risks – Credit Worthiness** – an assessment of the borrower's capacity and willingness, and past record, to repay loans. *In addition to their in-house expertise Banks get this input from various types of Credit Rating Agencies.*

- **Legal Risks – Legal Protection** – a strong legal system, comprising comprehensive laws and structure of enforcement, to be able to enforce contracts and recover their dues. *The continuous evolution of the Legal System under democratic political systems has been able to fulfill this need.*

- **Material Damage Risks – Asset Loss Protection** – a comprehensive system to obtain compensation for business assets and interests damaged by accidental occurrences. *The development of the Insurance Industry and its products provides the needed support.*

We are now in a position to summarize the strategic role played by the Insurance Industry in Economic Activity.

1. **Safety Net for Banking Industry**

   The Insurance Industry provides a vital 'Safety Net' for the Banking Industry. In the absence of an insurance policy, it would be very difficult, even impossible, for a Bank to recover loans advanced to finance assets and interests which may be damaged by accidental events. Without 'Insurance' Banking would become a much more risky venture.

2. **Growth Facilitator – Expansion of Industrial and Commercial Activity**

   Without the safety net provided by Insurance, Financial Institutions would be extremely reluctant to advance large loans, and the pace of industrial activity would be limited by the ability of the venture to raise its own funds internally. The Insurance Industry acts as a facilitator of economic growth.

3. **Financial Liquidity Facilitator – Capital Productivity Enhancer**

    Large amounts of capital would have to be kept aside in 'Sinking Funds' to provide for future losses. This would further reduce 'liquidity' in the financial system and create large pools of unproductive capital. Insurance enhances the productivity of capital by facilitating liquidity in the financial system.

4. **Risk Management Tool – Enterprise Stabilizer**

    Insurance acts as a useful risk management tool for enterprises and individuals. It helps them maintain the financial stability of organizations and individuals when they are faced with losses caused by accidental damages.

5. **Quality of Life Booster**

    The quality of life for individuals would also be adversely impacted. Today, an increasing number of individuals are able to fulfill their aspirations for a 'dwelling house' or a car of their dreams by taking loans from financial institutions. These loans are underpinned by insurance policies which protect the interest of the financial institution as a mortgagee in the event the asset itself is destroyed or damaged by an accident before the loan has been paid off. None of this would be possible without the protection provided by insurance policies.

We shall now proceed to examine the activity of Insurance and the associated basic concepts and principles in greater detail.

SECTION II

THE FOUNDATIONS OF INSURANCE
– Core Concepts, and Basic Principles

The previous three chapters would have helped the reader acquire a perspective about insurance as a tool for the management of 'risk' and its relationship with Banking in particular and the national Economy in general.

Chapters 4, 5 and 6 shall focus on presenting the basic 'Principles' of insurance, the mechanics through which the transfer of risk takes place and the foundational principles, the 'thumb' rules that guide this activity. They are meant to decode the rules used in decision making by practicing Managers as well as the Judicial Authorities which supervise the delivery of equity by the insurance system. The approach of the chapters is to continuously explain theories in the context of actual experience.

CHAPTER 4
Core Concepts

Core Concepts – Risk, Exposure, Peril, Hazard;
Types of Risk, Insurable and Uninsurable Risks

Up to this point we have arrived at a preliminary demarcation of the domain of General Insurance and the risks that arise within it. This is a rather broad understanding, based upon generalizations, to which more details must now be added.

Risk

In common usage the word 'risk' is used by people in several different ways. Sometimes it is used to refer to the 'chance' of a mishap, loss, damage, or some other harmful occurrence taking place. In this style of reference people speak of the 'high' or 'moderate' or 'low' risk of a road accident or theft taking place. At other times people, even Insurance or Risk Management professionals use it somewhat loosely to describe the property which is exposed to loss, say a house, a car, a factory or a person. It is also used to refer to the cause of a loss or event, such as 'fire,' 'storm,' 'short circuiting,' 'machinery breakdown,' or 'burglary.' All of this can be somewhat confusing, for in this manner the term 'Risk' is loosely used to refer to either the 'chance' of loss, or the 'property' or 'person' exposed to loss, or even to the 'cause' of loss. However, in the field or risk management in general, and especially in the context of insurance, the word risk has a very specific meaning.

Insurance is widely understood to involve the 'transfer' or 'sharing' of the risk of loss. What is transferred, or shared? It is the chance that a loss may occur which is shared, or transferred. In the context of insurance, the term 'risk' actually signifies 'chance' or 'possibility,' or 'probability' of an occurrence. You will note that when only one outcome is possible in a given set of conditions it is considered to be a 'certainty.' In contrast, when multiple outcomes are possible, we realize that there is a 'chance' or 'risk' that something may or may not occur. Risk then is the variation of the actual occurrence from the expected; it is the gap between what actually happens and the 'projection' or probability of what can happen. When there is no gap between the two we consider an event to be a certainty; everything else is a 'risk.' An event which is a 'certainty' cannot be insured; only risks are insurable, though, as we shall also discuss shortly, all risks cannot be insured. However, we can conclude with the observation that **'Risk'** is the chance or probability of occurrence of a loss, damage or injury.

Perils, Exposures and Hazards

The 'cause' of loss, in insurance terminology, is described as a **'Peril.'** The occurrence of the peril results in damage to some 'property,' or a loss to some 'interest,' or 'injury' to some person. For example, fire, lightning, storm, riots, burglary, accidental collision, are examples of perils.

The property or person, which may suffer the damage or loss, is described as an **'Exposure.'** A factory building, motor car, plant and machinery are examples of property. The term 'Exposure' can also be used to describe people such as the employees insured under a 'Group Health Insurance' policy or a Workmen's Compensations policy.

Conditions which occur and increase or reduce the chance or probability of the 'peril' occurring are called **'Hazard.'**

A small example will make the meaning of these terms more clear.

An acquaintance proposes to open a General Store in a newly constructed building in a part of town that is still not fully developed and settled. Though not many residents or commercial establishments have still moved into the area, he plans to use the 'early bird' advantage to capture business opportunities and corner market share. The store may not receive high 'foot falls' to begin with, but this could be a good opportunity. On the downside there is only one factor, the locality gets a little deserted after business hours and may not be very well policed yet.

How do we identify the various factors and concepts we just discussed? Your acquaintance is exposed to the possibility of a loss being caused by several factors. This 'possibility' of loss is the **risk.** It can be transferred, or protected, through an insurance policy.

The loss could be caused by several factors or perils. The occurrence of 'fire' could destroy the premises, the furniture and the stocks. Burglars could break in during the night and loot the store and the cash collected during the day. An earthquake could cause extensive damage. Remote as the possibility of these occurrences may seem, but they could wipe out the business. So the insurance policy would have to cover the **perils** of 'fire,' 'earthquake,' and 'burglary,' plus any others identified.

In this example, the term **'exposure'** denotes the building of the store, the stock of goods kept inside, the cash collected during the day and kept overnight inside the cash counter.

What of the 'Hazard'? Since the locality gets a little deserted after business hours the installation of CCTV Cameras and Burglar Alarm System, posting of a 'Watchman' or the institution of a 'Watch and Ward' operation are examples of improved hazard. They would improve the hazard. By keeping stocks of combustible goods such as 'fire crackers,' or 'kerosene,' or even of large quantities of edible oils, we would degrade the hazard. These would be examples of poor physical hazard.

At this stage we would like to mention that there are **three types of Hazard:**

- **Physical Hazard** refers to the physical and material conditions which increase the frequency or severity of a risk, e.g. under a motor insurance policy 'rain' would be a hazard which increases the risk of road accidents. Under a Fire Insurance policy, storage of combustible material or unshielded electric wiring would be examples of hazard, which increase the chances of loss by fire.

- **Moral Hazard** refers to conditions relating to the intentions, the integrity of persons in such a way that it makes the transfer of risk, or the contract of insurance inequitable, unfair or dishonest. Intentionally giving wrong information at the time of entering into the insurance contract, or while making a claim, with the intention of inflating the claim, and getting more benefit than is legitimately due, is an example of moral hazard. In simple terms all examples of dishonesty in intentions and actions would be examples of moral hazard.

- **Morale Hazard** also refers to intentions or conditions, not to outright dishonesty, but to negligence or indifference to a risk. For example, driving too fast, breaking the speed limit, being careless about leaving the keys inside a parked car, or not checking all the locks and latches on doors and windows before leaving the premises at the end of a business day are all illustrative of 'morale hazard.'

Types of Risks; Insurable and Uninsurable Risks

We can now round off our understanding of these core concepts by identifying different types of risks and which types are insurable and which uninsurable. Though there are quite a large number of ways to classifying risks for our purposes there are four distinct types of pairs:

Pure & Speculative Risks

- **Pure Risks** are those where the occurrence of something leads to a loss, but where the absence, or the not occurring of that thing does not lead to a profit but only maintains the status quo. For example, the occurrence of fire or burglary or a road accident, are categorized as 'pure risks.' Their occurrence only produces a loss, but if these do not occur that does not lead to a better or profitable situation. That only leaves you where you were, no better, or worse.

- **Speculative Risks** are those where the occurrence of something could lead to a profit or a loss, or even a break-even situation. For example, investing on the stock market, or 'gambling' are 'speculative' risks. Stock Market movements could lead to profits, or losses, or a no-profit-nor-loss situation. The same goes for gambling, for you could win, or loose, and though this happens rarely, find that at the end you had the same amount of money as when you started.

Pure Risks can be insured, but Speculative Risks are considered uninsurable.

Fundamental & Particular Risks

- **Fundamental Risks** are those which affect very large groups. They have an effect on all the members of a group. They are caused by social, economic or political factors which operate on the national, or even, an international level. For example, 'economic risks,' such as government policies, the establishment or termination of trade relationships between two nations, the creation of special economic zones or industrial clusters in a particular geographical area are all risks which have an effect on very large groups of people, and on all of them. The occurrence of war, or of a nuclear explosion or breakdown, is also considered a Fundamental Risk. The impact of Fundamental Risks is considered to be too widespread, or catastrophic, and this makes them unsuitable for treatment by commercial entities. They are left to be managed by governmental action.

- **Particular Risks** are such that their occurrence affects only a few people, small groups or even a single individual, but not the sort of large groups which are affected by Fundamental Risks. Fire, Burglary, Riots and Strikes, Storms, floods, and Earthquakes are regarded as Particular Risks. These risks are considered suitable for insurance by commercial entities such as Insurance Companies.

Since Storms, Floods, and Earthquakes, and similar natural catastrophes, also affect very large numerical and geographically spread out groups, some may argue that they should also be regarded as 'fundamental risks.' However, historically, the Insurance Industry has offered insurance protection against damages caused by storms, floods and earthquakes. It will also be observed that though some of these events have disastrous consequences, yet their impact varies in scope and spread, and is perhaps not on the same scale as some of the risk classified above as 'fundamental.'

Static & Dynamic Risks

- **Static Risks** are said to be those which could arise irrespective of changes at an institutional or group level, such as changes in the economy; for example losses arising from natural events such as floods, or caused by the dishonest dealings of employees, are examples of static risks.

- **Dynamic Risks** are those which result from institutional or group level changes. An example of these would be changes in prices, which may happen at the local, city or even state level. Changes in consumer tastes, fashion trends, technology are other examples.

Broadly speaking, whereas static risks are amenable to treatment and mitigation through insurance dynamic risks are not insured.

Sometimes two more types of risk are spoken of. These are financial & non-financial risks and subjective and objective risks.

Financial & Non-Financial Risks

- **Financial Risks** are considered to be those where the loss can be quantified.

- **Non-Financial Risks** are those where the loss cannot be quantified no matter how severe its impact may be on the person who suffers the loss.

Subjective & Objective Risks

- **Subjective Risks** arise from an individual's perceptions, psychological state or attitudes. They occur because of an individual's perception of the effect of an event, whether it would be beneficial or harmful. Such a risk and its effects cannot be quantified and measured. These risks cannot be insured.

- **Objective Risks** are those which can be observed, quantified and measured. The probability of their occurrence can be predicted through either deductive reasoning (by using the theory of probability) or through inductive reasoning methods (actuarial calculations based on observation of data sets, experimental data, samples). Objective risks are usually considered to be fit for insurance.

From the short analysis presented above it will be apparent that Insurers do not, and cannot, insure all risks. What types of risks are insurable? Generally speaking, risks which are of the type described as pure, particular, financial and objective are appropriate for management through insurance. However, some risks which are catastrophic, and have widespread effect in the same way as fundamental risks do, such as floods and earthquakes, are accepted by Insurers, but by and large the rule of thumb hold good and speculative, fundamental, non-financial and subjective risks are considered uninsurable.

CHAPTER 5
The Mechanics of Insurance

The Mechanics of Insurance – the structured activity of risk transfer,
the mechanism and how it operates; Proposer, Insured and Insurer;
the Pool and Portfolios – lines of business; The Sales Process, the Contract, Offer,
Acceptance and Consideration, the Premium; The Claims Process,
Claim Intimation & Registration, Loss Survey & Assessment,
Claim Disbursement

The Structured Transfer of Risk

In our exploration of the subject of insurance we have arrived at a functional understanding of it as an act of risk management where the risk of loss faced by individuals is shared or transferred to a larger group. This is done with the intention of reducing or eliminating the impact of losses for the few who suffer them by getting the larger 'group' to share them. We also explored core concepts such as risk, peril, exposure and hazard, finally reaching the point of recognizing the distinction between insurable and uninsurable risks. Before we go any further we must acquaint ourselves with how the transfer of risk actually takes place. This is a small, but necessary, diversion into the mundane world of processes before we return to the domain of concepts.

Try to visualize two people, one of who wishes to share, or transfer to the other, his risk of sending a cargo of Leather Coats made at his factory in Agra, Uttar Pradesh, to a buyer in Bangalore, Karnataka. The two would need to settle a lot of conditions of the 'What if" sort, about the type of contingencies and losses which are covered by their agreement, and their mutual rights and duties. In addition a good deal of hard bargaining would take place over the cost of the sharing of risk. In the end all the relevant details would have to be written in a document recording their contract, which would have to conform to the existing laws. And if, for any reason, the two could not agree on everything, the owner of the cargo would have to start the process all over again with a new person. Somewhat like a transaction of the 'Barter Trade' type. Quite a task you would agree. In the early days of Insurance, perhaps two thousand or more years ago till the 18th century

CE, the transactions were conducted in this manner between individuals who would gather together in some common meeting place. Today, nobody would find it worthwhile to even attempt such 'barter' style transactions. Insurance has now become a highly structured business, the markets for which are still mostly confined within national boundaries, but which has global linkages and impact. It is governed both by the general laws of contract, and also by a specific body of laws and conventions which have a very high degree of international consensus and acceptance behind it. How is the business conducted today? Listed below are the important components of the insurance universe. These are the 'Roles,' 'Transactions,' 'Business Instruments' through the interplay of which the business is conducted.

The Proposer: The Entity, or Person, which wishes to transfer or share its risk is called the 'Proposer.' *The sharing of risks is not a direct exchange or 'mutual' activity conducted between entities and persons who wish to share or transfer their risk.*

The Insurer: The transfer or Risk is conducted through the intermediation of an Insurance Company, also called an 'Insurer,' which maintains and administers a large, common 'pool' of similar risks. The Insurer is only the custodian of the pool and not its owner.

Portfolio: A 'pool' of similar risks maintained by the Insurer is called a 'Portfolio.' The Insurance Act of 1938, is the primary legislation governing the conduct of insurance business in India. It classifies general insurance into three 'classes of 'business,' Fire, Marine and Miscellaneous. For an insurance company in India each of these classes of business constitutes the primary 'pool' or 'portfolio.'[2]

Line-of-Business is a popular term used to describe a sub-category within the three main portfolios mentioned as business under the Insurance Act of 1938.

The Insured: The Entity or Person who is the policyholder is called the 'Insured.' Therefore, we can say that the Insured is that Proposer whose proposal to surrender risk is accepted by the Insurer, resulting in the issue of a policy of insurance. In other words, when the Proposer's 'offer' to surrender a risk is accepted by the Insurer, and a Policy of insurance is issued, then the Proposer becomes the 'Insured' under the policy.

Underwriting: The Underwriter is the specialist, usually an employee of an Insurance Company, who is authorized to evaluate an insurance proposal, decide if it should be accepted, and on what terms, conditions and premium.

The Sales Process – *consisting of the steps of Invitation, Offer-Proposal, Counter Offer-Quotation, Consideration-Premium, Acceptance-Receipt, culminating in the Contract-Policy*

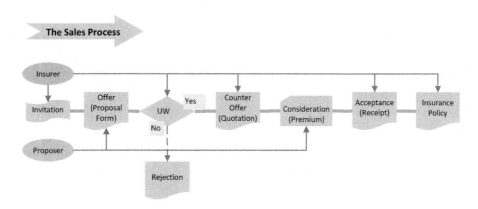

Figure 3: The Sales Process

The Invitation: the Invitation-to-Offer signifies all the publicity material, Advertisements, Brochure, and Prospectus which is issued by the Insurer to provide product information to the public.

Offer: The Proposal Form is a structured questionnaire issued by an Insurer to a prospective customer or buyer who is required to fill it up and submit it to the Insurer. It contains detailed information about the risk, exposure and coverage required. When the Proposal Form is submitted to the Insurer it acts as the Proposer's 'Offer' to share or surrender his risk to the pool through the Insurer.

Counter Offer: The Insurer may reject the 'Offer.' Alternatively, he may decide to accept it in part, or full, and state the specific terms and conditions, and the required payment or consideration for accepting the offer. The 'Quotation' of Premium is the document issued by the Insurer which records the terms, conditions and amount of payment required by it for accepting the risk. This is the counter offer made by the Insurer to the Proposer.

Consideration: The amount of money which the Insurer demands from the Proposer for accepting the latter's offer to share specified risk is mentioned in the Quotation. This amount is the 'Consideration' which the Proposer must pay. In insurance terminology it is called the 'Premium.' The payment can be made either in cash or by cheque, or remitted through the electronic mode by Credit Card or Debit Card.

Acceptance: When the Proposer accepts the terms contained in the Quotation and remits the Premium demanded under it, the Insurer must record the remittance of 'consideration' by issuing a 'Premium Receipt.' This is the Insurer's 'Acceptance' of the 'Offer' of the 'Risk' by the Proposer. By Law, in India, no Insurer can accept any risk before the premium has been paid by the Proposer.[3]

Contract: The 'Acceptance' of the 'Offer' and the successful remittance and acceptance of the 'Consideration' results in the establishment of a 'Contract' between the Insurer and the Proposer who is now called the 'Insured' under the contract of insurance. The 'Contract' of insurance is called an 'Insurance Policy, or 'policy' in short. The Insurance Policy is issued by the Insurer, and is based upon the facts recorded in the Proposal Form and the Quotation. It must reflect in letter and spirit the features and details mentioned in the various components of the 'Invitation' publicized by the Insurer.

The Insurance Claim: When the Insured suffers a loss, due to damage or destruction of the exposure insured by a policy, then he is entitled to recover this loss from the Insurer under the contractual terms of his policy. The Insured's demand on the Insurer for payment of compensation for a loss, based upon the terms of the insurance contract, is called a 'Claim' under the policy.

The Claims Process

Whenever an Insured makes a Claim under his policy, the Insurer is faced with two important issues or questions. The First Question concerns the nature of loss. It has to be determined what caused the loss, how it occurred, and whether it is payable under the contract. The Second Question relates to the extent of damage and the exact amount of compensation payable for it. The Claims Process is organized with the objective of establishing answers to both these questions so that the Insurer can take an objective decision on his duty under the contract. In short, whether the claim is payable, and for what amount are the twin issues at stake.

Claim Intimation: The Insured must immediately inform the Insurer about the occurrence of an event that has resulted in a loss that is covered by the terms of the policy. This is a formal communication of information which is usually done in writing, but increasingly, it can be also done through email or a telephone call to a designated recipient. This 'Intimation' of a loss to the Insurer is the formal demand by the Insured for payment of compensation by the Insurer, under the terms of the contract of insurance. The 'Intimation' is the formal step by which the Insured 'invokes' the contract.

The Claim Form: Insurers usually prefer that the 'Intimation' of a claim is done through the submission of a 'Claim Form' by the Insured. Even when the information is conveyed through a letter, email or telephone call, they insist that this document is eventually submitted to complete the process. *Some Insurers accept Claim Intimations without the submission of a Claim Form. They proceed with the process of Claim Registration, leaving the submission of the Claim Form for* *a later date, sometimes even at the Loss Assessment stage.* The Claim Form is a structured questionnaire for obtaining specific information about the loss in a systematic manner. This information is vital for subsequent steps by which the claim is processed.

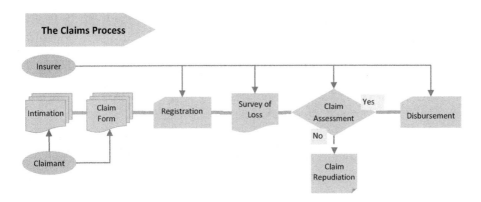

Figure 4: The Claims Process

Claim Registration: The process for intimation of a claim is completed when the Insurer formally registers it in their business books, and then issues a unique reference number called 'Claim Number.' In this way the Insurer makes a formal acknowledgement that the Insured has invoked the contract. It now becomes the contractual duty of the Insurer to quantify the loss and discharge his liability under its terms.

Survey of Loss: The Survey is a series of acts of inspection of the damage to the exposure and enquiries related to it. It is done with two main objectives. Firstly, it is vital to determine the actual cause of the loss, and establish whether this was covered or included in the contract. Secondly the exact extent of loss has to be quantified in monetary terms. The Survey is conducted by domain specialists who are professionally qualified and licensed to conduct loss assessments for insurance claims. These professionals are called 'Surveyors' by the insurance fraternity. The Surveyor, after completing the survey, submits a formal 'Survey Report' to the Insurer giving his findings on the cause of loss and the amount of damage sustained.

Assessment of Claim: On the basis of the Survey Report the Insurer takes a decision on the two important issues:

Firstly, whether the claim is payable and the demand for compensation is valid under the terms of the contract, or should liability under the contract be denied, or repudiated?

Secondly, what is the amount payable as claim?

Disbursement: If the assessment of the claims results in a decision to accept the claim then the amount assessed is disbursed to the Insured, who is also often referred to as the 'Claimant' in connection with the claim.

The Claims Manager is the employee who is given the responsibility to coordinate the conduct of the Claims Process and take decisions on behalf of the Insurer about payment of claims.

Our survey of the core concepts and the mechanics of insurance has provided an overall perspective of how the business of insurance functions to complete which we must examine the basic principles of insurance.

Over a period of time the adjudication of disputes by law courts has created a body of common law and a set of interpretations which is now globally accepted. This has resulted in the evolution of five basic principles which are widely regarded as the foundation of insurance business and contracts. These basic principles of insurance do not contradict or conflict with the general principles of contract law, but suitably modify them according to the specific context of insurance business, and we will now examine them and their application in detail.

CHAPTER 6
Insurance Dynamics

Basic Principles; Insurable Interest; Utmost Good Faith; Proximate Cause;
Indemnity; Sum Insured, Market Value and Depreciation;
Condition of Average and Under-Insurance; Contribution and Subrogation

The Basic Principles of Insurance

The Basic Principles of Insurance can be viewed as answers to four basic questions or issues, which if they were to be summarized in a single word each, could be called the questions of 'Who,' 'How Much,' ' When and Why,' 'What.'

First, we are confronted by the question of 'Who'? Who can take an insurance policy? Can *'Anyone' or only the Owner of a property purchase insurance? Or, can 'Others' who claim to be affected also do so?* Who, then, is entitled to collect compensation for a loss insured by an Insurance Policy? The answer to this question is called the **'Principle of Insurable Interest.'**

Second, before us is the question of 'How much'? For how much value should insurance be taken, and for what value would the compensation be paid. Is there a relationship between the value insured and the amount paid as compensation? The **'Principle of Indemnity,'** and its' corollary, the **'Principle of Subrogation and Contribution'** provide the answer.

Third, the question arises whether any and every loss is payable under a policy? 'Which' losses are payable? In what circumstances' is a loss not payable under the contract? Is short, why is a particular loss payable, and another not payable. The answer to this dilemma is provided by the **'Principle of Proximate Cause.'**

Fourth, what must the Insured and Insurer do to uphold the spirit of their contract? It is well known that all contracts are founded on 'Good Faith.' Yet, contracts of insurance are somewhat different, and given their unique features, the contracting parties are bound by reciprocal rights and duties which go beyond the requirements of 'good faith' demanded under ordinary contracts. The conduct of the Insured and Insurer must be based on 'Utmost Good Faith.' The **'Principle** of Utmost Good Faith' lays down the guiding operational principle behind their various reciprocal rights and duties.

At one glance these questions appear quite simple, and their answers obvious, and neither would seem to require consideration at any great length. A little bit of 'common sense' is all that seems to be required to provide solutions. Yet, as the saying goes, 'Common Sense is anything but common,' and often events are a jumble of occurrences not easy to segregate and disentangle into distinct features. Basic Principles, common sense, rigorous application of logic, and established business conventions provide the basis for correct decisions. We shall now discuss these 'Basic Principles' in detail.

The Principle of Insurable Interest

Consider the first question posed a little earlier. Who can buy an insurance policy? It is tempting to offer the immediate response that anyone could buy one if they were willing to pay for it. That is correct, but only part of the truth. If we keep the 'purpose' of insurance in mind, the answer to this question becomes obvious.

The purpose of insurance is to offer financial protection against an accidental loss. Who would suffer a loss if some property were damaged? Obviously the 'Owner' of the property would stand to lose. In addition so would any person who has the responsibility for its safety and maintenance, or a contractual duty to compensate the owner for its loss. Such a person is called a 'Bailee.' Likewise a Bank or Financial Institution may have mortgaged the property and advanced a loan against it to the owner, and they too would suffer a loss if the property were damaged and the owner unable to pay back the loan. The Bank or Financial Institution are 'Mortgagors' and have an insurable interest to the extent of their loan. Owners, Bailees and Mortgagors are said to have an 'Insurable Interest' in specific property which can be protected through insurance.

We can define Insurable Interest as "the interest of a person in some property, life or asset where damage or loss to such property, life or asset would lead to a financial loss to the person, and the continued preservation of the same would result in financial benefit."

A few examples will help illustrate the meaning of Insurable interest better. A person who buys a Car, or inherits a house has an insurable interest in it as the legal owner. Other family members may benefit from the use of the asset, may be emotionally attached to it, but have no 'insurable interest' as they have no legal relationship with it and would not suffer any financial loss if it were damaged.

A parent bears legal and financial responsibility for their dependent children, and therefore has insurable interest in their health and wellbeing. The parent therefore has an insurable interest in the children which can be protected through insurance. Similarly, an individual has an insurable interest in their spouse.

An employer, whether a small shop owner or a large industrial conglomerate, is responsible for the safety of his employees while at work. Employers are also liable at law to compensate employees for injuries or deaths suffered during the course of employment, and therefore have an insurable interest in the person of their employees.

Not just the Owner, but even a Tenant or Licensee, conceivably, has an insurable interest in the property occupied by them under the terms of a contractual agreement which holds them responsible for the continued maintenance of the occupied property and its eventual return in good condition to the owner. The tenant who occupies a house, or a hirer who uses a machine, may become liable to pay for the accidental damages to the rented or hired property. This creates an interest, the contractual responsibility, which can be insured against specified accidental damages.

To summarize, anyone who will suffer a financial loss if the insured asset is damaged or destroyed, is said to have an 'Insurable Interest' in it, and can take an insurance policy to protect it. In addition, someone who is responsible for the maintenance and safety of the property and can be held liable if it is destroyed, with a responsibility to pay compensation, has an insurable interest in the property at least to the extent of his liability.

The Principle of Indemnity

The idea behind the principle of Indemnity can be best understood if we remember the basic purpose of insurance which is to provide adequate compensation for a loss. A person who suffers a loss must be restored to the same financial position in which he was placed before the loss occurred. Insurance professionals like to say that the objective of insurance is to "make good the loss." The loss, it is said, should be reimbursed in full, but no one should make a profit from the loss, by gaining an amount that is greater than the value of the loss suffered. Equally, the purpose is not achieved if someone only gets partial compensation. Then, the idea of insurance itself would have failed, since that individual would have suffered a loss despite the activity of 'insuring' the risk. Therefore, Indemnity can be described as adequate compensation, which creates neither a profit nor a loss for the Insured. We are now in a good position to formulate a definition of the principle of indemnity.

The Principle of Indemnity states that through the medium of insurance, an Insured should be able to obtain such measure of compensation that he is restored to the same financial position as he was in before the event of loss occurred, achieving in the end neither a profit nor a loss as result of the mishap.

The principle of indemnity is one of the five pillars which together uphold the edifice of insurance, but by itself it is not enough to achieve the goal of adequate compensation. Think of a situation in which an Insured person first obtained the full compensation from the Insurance Company, and then proceeded to sue the person who had caused the damage. He would be entitled to sue under the Law of Torts, and the Courts may award him some amount as Damages. If this were to happen then this Insured person would have got not only the full compensation from the Insurance Company, but also some additional compensation through legal action. Over and above all this, the Insured could also sell the 'Salvage' which is the scrap or damaged item for whatever value it could fetch. All told, he would have received more than he lost, and would now be making a profit. This is something which is against the objective of insurance. The Principle of Subrogation is designed to prevent this from happening.

The Principle of Subrogation and Contribution

Subrogation

Subrogation should be described as the legal right of one person, after having indemnified another person due to a contractual obligation to do so, to stand in the place of the latter and avail of all the rights and remedies of the latter, whether enforced or not. Therefore, Subrogation lies in assuming the legal rights of a person for whom expenses or a debt has been paid. The person who pays for the damages of some other also automatically acquires all the rights and obligations which the latter person had regarding the damaged property.

Typically, in insurance, subrogation occurs when an insurance company pays a claim to the Insured, or admits liability to pay it. The Insurance Company is now said to be 'subrogated' to the rights of the claimant. It has now automatically got the legal right to sue and recover whatever was due to the Insured from any third parties who may have been responsible for the loss. The Insurance Company also has the right to take over the damaged property, or 'salvage,' and sell it to realize the best price possible

In legal terms, the Insurance Company is the *Subrogee,* while the Insured is the *Subrogor,* and the person responsible for the damage, and who has to be sued, is the *Tortfeasor*.

The operation of subrogation will become clearer through the example below.

Example: *ABC Ltd., Mumbai, sends cargo to its buyer XYZ Ltd., Chennai, by Road, through TUV Ltd., a Road Transport Company. ABC Ltd. takes In-land Transit All-Risks Cargo Insurance from RGIC, Mumbai. The Cargo is delivered in a damaged condition. XYZ Ltd., which refuses to accept damaged goods and asks ABC to replace the damaged items. ABC has suffered a loss, and it makes a claim on RGIC under its' policy. Now ABC has a legal right to recover damages from the carrier TUV Ltd. RGIC will pay the claim to ABC, and then, by the law of Subrogation, all the rights of ABC accrue to RGIC, which will be entitled to recover due amount from the Carrier, TUV Ltd.*

The principle of Subrogation states that after a claim has been paid or liability to pay it has been accepted under the contract of insurance, the Insurance Company becomes entitled to all the rights and remedies which were originally available to the Insured, whether to sue and recover damages from third parties responsible for the loss or to sell the damaged article as salvage.

The law of subrogation takes care of one loophole which could have resulted in a claimant legally earning profit out of a loss. Due to the act of Subrogation the right to recover damages and sell salvage belongs to the Insurance Company after it has paid a claim to the Insured. Without the operation of 'Subrogation' the Claimant would be able to sell the Salvage and recover 'Damages' through legal process even after having collected full compensation from the Insurer. The amount collected as salvage and for damages would be a profit over and above the sum received as compensation. However, one more loophole still remains. What if an insured takes multiple policies from different companies to cover the same property against the same risks? For example, suppose the owner of a small garment factory decides to insure the factory building valued at one crore rupees (INR 1,00,00,000/-) by taking four different policies from different companies. Each policy insures the building for one crore. If the factory building was totally destroyed, the factory's owner would be in a position to collect a claim of one crore under each of the four policies and walk away with a sum of four crore rupees against a loss of only one crore, except for the Principle of Contribution.

Contribution

The 'Contribution' condition which is a part of all insurance policies is a corollary to the Principle of indemnity. In its absence an insured could obtain more than one policy covering the same risk, and he would be able to recover the same loss from more than one source. The Contribution condition stops this from happening. It ensures that each policy pays only a portion of the loss that is equal to its share of the total value of insurance by all the policies. Otherwise a Insured could recover multiple amounts from different policies and would wind up making a profit, out of a calamity like a loss. This would defeat the spirit and purpose of Insurance.

The example of the Garment Factory can be used to illustrate the workings of the principle of 'Contribution.' *The Owner had taken out four Fire Insurance policies A and B for Rs.1,00,00,000/- (one crore) each, and C and D for Rs. 50,00,000/- (fifty lac each) to insure the factory building. The building was damaged by fire causing a loss of Rs. 24,75,000/- (twenty four lac and seventy five thousand). In the absence of the Contribution Condition it would be possible for the Insured to collect Rs. 24,75,000/- from each of the four policies. This would result in his getting a total of Rs. 99,00,000/- (ninety nine lac) against an actual loss that was only Rs. 24,75,000/- (twenty four lac and seventy five thousand).*

Due to the operation of the condition of Contribution the four policies shall together pay a total of Rs. 24,75,000/- (twenty four lac and seventy five thousand) in the following way:

Table 1: An Illustration of Contribution between Policies – Apportionment of Loss

LOSS (L) = 24,75,000/-			
Policy	Sum Insured	Ratable Portion	Share of Loss
A	AS = 1,00,00,000.00	AS/ES = 1/3	AC = L x 1/3 =8,25,000/-
B	BS = 1,00,00,000.00	BS/ES = 1/3	BC = L x 1/3 =8,25,000/-
C	CS= 50,00,000.00	CS/ES = 1/6	CC = L x 1/6 =4,12,500/-
D	DS= 50,00,000.00	DS/ES = 1/6	DC = L x 1/3 =4,12,500/-
E [TOTAL]	ES = 3,00,00,000.00		24,75,000/-

We can now define the principle of Contribution is a few words.

The Principle of Contribution states that if a risk is insured under multiple policies against the same perils then each policy shall pay only a ratable portion of the loss, the ratable portion being in the same proportion to the loss as the Sum Insured by each policy bears to the Total Sum Insured by all the policies.

The Principle of Proximate Cause

Usually most people do not find it difficult to think of a 'cause' for events and actions they come across in their daily lives. In fact human beings are conditioned by years of habit and education to believe that nothing happens without a reason and everything has a cause. They view their lives through the cause-effect paradigm, and with a little effort can usually come up with a probable cause, right or wrong, for what happens around them. People sometimes say they missed a train or could not catch a flight because they got caught in a traffic jam. In their view the 'Traffic jam' is the cause for the missed flight. Yet, in a different view, it is not the traffic jam but the lack of adequate planning to account for such eventualities, the last minute delays or detours, which could be the reason for not reaching the airport on time. Sometimes it is quite easy, and at others quite difficult, to tell the real cause for what happened as we shall see a little later in this discussion.

It is important to know the real 'cause' for both good and harmful actions, if for no other reason then, at least to ensure that mistakes are not repeated and the right actions are always taken. In terms of the business of insurance it is vital to know with certainty the 'real' or 'actual' cause for any particular event that leads to a loss. Losses that are caused by perils insured by an insurance policy are payable to the policyholder, and It is therefore important to establish a simple and unambiguous methodology for determining the cause of loss or event. We need a defined, universally accepted, way of deciding upon the 'cause.' This need is fulfilled by the principle of 'Proximate Cause.'

The classical definition of 'Proximate Cause' describes it as the active and efficient cause that produces, without the intervention of any other cause, an unbroken chain of events that culminate in the occurrence of the said event or loss. While pronouncing judgment in the legal case of Pawsey v Scottish Union & National Insurance Company (1908) Proximate Cause was defined as:

"The active and efficient cause that sets in motion a train of events which brings about a result, without the intervention of any force started and working actively from a new and independent source."[4]

This formulation of the concept, though originating in English Law, has been universally accepted globally. It consists of the following distinct components: firstly, an 'efficient' cause, or one which is responsible for or instrumental for what happens; secondly the event itself or the unbroken chain of events which is the effect or final event; and thirdly, the absence in this causal chain of any intervention by some other act or event which has its origins in a different source. We shall now use this definition to help us determine the proximate cause in two different situations.

In the first case, over a dozen shops were gutted by a blaze that spread quickly and destroyed property worth a few crore of rupees. It was widely accepted that the fire originated in a General Store, possibly due to a carelessly thrown cigarette butt that fell on some waste packing material lying in a corner. Being highly combustible in nature this ignited quickly, and before anyone could realize it the fire spread to a drum of kerosene kept nearby. After this there was no stopping it and the fire swiftly engulfed the garment shops situated on either side of the General Store. Garments catch fire quite easily and burn strongly, and the blaze had spread before the Fire Brigade managed to control it. In this example it is not difficult to identify the proximate cause of the fire which destroyed the General Store. The carelessly thrown cigarette butt was the proximate cause. Even if the fire in each shop is treated as a separate and distinct event, the proximate cause for each shop, other than the General Store, can be easily identified as the fire which was burning in the neighbouring store.

Next, consider a slightly more complex example. A man got up late in the morning. He had been working till late the night before, had finished some important work and wanted to reach his workplace early next morning to deliver the output. In the little time that he had he knew that he had to rush and somehow catch a train. As he reached the railway platform he saw a train about to depart and began to run to catch it. The surface of the platform was slippery for it has rained a little while ago and in his hurry the man lost his footing on the rain slicked surface. He twisted his ankle, fell down and broke his arm. The two injuries he suffered, a twisted ankle and a broken arm were the result of his fall on a slippery surface. Did he slip because he lost his footing, or because the surface was slippery? Was he a little less careful because he was in a hurry? What caused him to get up late that morning? Could he have finished his work more quickly in the night, and could he have got up a little earlier than he did? Was it 'work' or laziness that lay at the root of his lack of time? The questions and possible answers, the permutation and combination of possible factors is extremely large. The concept of proximate cause simplifies the whole issue of what caused the injuries. It was the loss of footing which caused the man to fall down and injure himself. The slippery nature of the surface, the rainfall which made it slippery, the man's need to hurry and catch the train, may have added to the hazard and to the probability of a man losing his footing, but they are in the nature of independent sources or factors and cannot be considered 'active' or 'efficient' causes of the injuries. The act of accidentally slipping is the 'active' and 'efficient' cause that started the train of events which resulted in the man falling down and injuring himself. This is the proximate cause.

The concept of 'proximate cause' is very logical and fairly straight forward, and you may well wonder why an elaborate or formal definition of it is required at all. In fact there is a very good reason why such a definition is required. You will notice that more often than not individuals tend to blame something, anything, at times even everything, for whatever goes wrong. Usually this is a subjective exercise, a type of 'blame game.' For instance, in the second example mentioned above, people could consider 'over work and fatigue,' 'lack of adequate rest,' 'haste,' 'slippery surface' as root causes for the injuries. 'Cause' means different things to different people, but it is important to eliminate subjectivity from the process of decision making. At times, real life situations can also be more complex than these simple examples, and multiple factors can function at the same time to produce an event which is a chain of occurrences that are not easy to segregate. In such situations it becomes all the more necessary to deploy a standardized definition. A definition provides a standardized and universally accepted methodology for determining the 'cause' for a loss, and helps us take a balanced and objective decision whether a particular loss is payable or not under the contract of insurance.

The Principle of Utmost Good Faith

All Contracts are based on the observance of 'Good Faith' between the contracting parties. Any action performed by any contracting party, which amounts to a breach or violation of the requirements of 'good faith' vitiates the contract, and gives the aggrieved party the right to withdraw from all or some of its obligations, or even repudiate the contract altogether. What is this duty of 'Good Faith' enjoined on the parties to a contract? The contracting parties, a seller and a buyer, are expected to promise what they intend, and to do what they promise. They must be of the same mind (consensus ad idem), and must give each other adequate and accurate information about their part of the transaction under the contract. In other words, they must give each other correct information, and fair opportunity to enquire into the facts. But, what are the limits or boundaries of this duty? The limits are set by the classic dictum of 'caveat emptor,' which literally means 'let the buyer beware.' Sections 18 and 19 of the Indian Contract Act throw clear light on how caveat emptor operates in practice.[5] While presenting adequate and accurate information a party is exempted from providing information, or even excused for providing incomplete information, about something which the other party is commonly expected to know or has the opportunity to independently find out. In simpler terms, if there is something which any buyer is commonly expected to know, or can easily find out through inspection and enquiry, then it is not necessary for a seller to provide that information. If the seller does not provide the buyer with complete information, or provides information which may not be completely accurate, but provides the buyer with full opportunity to obtain and verify such information, then he will have satisfied his duty of "Good Faith."[6] Truly the buyer must 'beware.' Good faith requires all parties to achieve common understanding and intention, on the basis of information freely and fairly exchanged about facts which are either in the public domain or can be easily verified by them. Lack of Good Faith, or bad faith, arises when one party presents incomplete or incorrect information in a situation where the other parties are denied the opportunity or do not have the opportunity to fairly and independently verify it.

Insurance Contracts however require the parties to observe not just good faith, but 'Utmost Good faith.' Why? And, how is this to be achieved? Why is the condition of Good Faith adequate for all other types of contracts, but needs to be transformed into 'utmost good faith' when it comes to insurance contracts? Under an insurance contract there is a condition of information asymmetry. The 'Insured' or buyer of insurance knows much more about the risk, the history of loss experience, the condition of the property at risk, than the Insurer. Often the insurer may be at a distant location without any opportunity of physically inspecting the property, or knowing the exact conditions of, and hazard to which it is exposed. The Insurer has perforce to depend upon facts revealed to him by the Insured or Proposer as he is called at this stage of the transaction. The responsibility to provide adequate and accurate information in an insurance transaction rests even more firmly and heavily on the Insured than it would on a seller or buyer under an ordinary commercial contract. The Proposer, or Insured, must disclose to the Insurer all material facts that he knows or is expected to know, which would influence the decision of a prudent insurer to accept the risk and determine its pricing. A material fact is all information of the type which acts as a criterion for acceptance of risk by the Insurer and the price at which they would do so. The insurers, who issue the contract document, have the same duty to observe utmost good faith while issuing the policy and should ensure that there is no ambiguity in the contract wording and all conditions are adequately revealed to the Insured.

The essence of 'Utmost Good Faith' was perhaps first, and best, enunciated by Lord Mansfield, an English Judge from the 18th century while pronouncing judgment in the leading and often quoted case of Carter v Boehm (1766) 97 ER 1162, 1164. The Judge observed that

"Insurance is a contract of speculation... The special facts, upon which the contingent chance is to be computed, lie most commonly in the knowledge of the insured only: the under-writer trusts to his representation, and proceeds upon confidence that he does not keep back any circumstances in his knowledge, to mislead the under-writer into a belief that the circumstance does not exist... Good faith forbids either party by concealing what he privately knows, to draw the other into a bargain from his ignorance of that fact, and his believing the contrary."[7]

The Insured must disclose to the Insurer all 'material' facts. He must not withhold, deny, suppress information or misrepresent facts. The Insurer, who draws up the contract, must ensure that the policy is free from ambiguity in covering the risk in the same manner in which the Insured proposes to cover it. In simple words, 'no window dressing of facts' by the Insured and 'no sugar coating of the conditions'/ 'no fine print in the policy' by the Insurer must guide their contractual relationship. Non-disclosure or misrepresentation by the Insured make the policy void or voidable, and would allow the Insurer to not pay a claim. Similarly, any ambiguity in the policy conditions would result in the benefit of the doubt going to the Insured.

Table 2: Basic Principles – Q & AC

Principle	Issue (Question)	Resolution (Answer)
Insurable Interest	*Who?* Who can take an insurance policy for an asset or person?	*An Owner, Bailee or Mortgagor!* Anyone who will suffer a financial loss if the insured asset is damaged or destroyed, or if an insured person is injured or dies.
Indemnity	How Much Value? The Policy should be taken for what value? And, how much Compensation will be received?	*Adequate to Compensate!* The value should be such that Insured neither makes a profit nor a loss, but is restored to the same position as before the loss.
Subrogation	Who has the right to seek 'damages' before a Court of Law? Who can sell the salvage?	After payment of claim, or admission of liability, the Insurer has the right to sell Salvage and receive 'Damages' awarded by a Court.
Contribution	Can an Insured collect compensation for the same loss under multiple Policies? If 'Yes,' then how much?	Insured can collect compensation under multiple policies each of which will contribute no more than their proportionate share to payment of claim so that total payment does not lead to a 'profit.'

Contd.

Proximate Cause	What is the real cause? When multiple factors, or causes, seem to have operated sequentially, or concurrently, and contributed to the event causing loss, then which is the 'real' cause?	The immediate, active and efficient cause for which leads to an event without intervention of any other factor is the 'Proximate' or real cause!
Utmost Good Faith	What is required to Remove 'Information asymmetry' between the Proposer and Insurer about the nature and state of property, and about the terms and conditionalities of the Insurance policy.	Disclosure of all 'material facts' by Proposer and complete information of all conditions and elimination of all ambiguities from Policy wordings by Insurer will create a 'consensus' of intent
	What information should be exchanged, and action taken, by the Proposer (Insured) and Insurer to ensure that the Insurance Contract is based on full knowledge and mutual understanding of facts and the terms and conditions applicable to the contract?	The Proposer must make a full declaration of all facts that could influence the Insurer's decision to accept or decline the proposal or determine premium rates, and secondly, by the Insurer ensuring that there are no ambiguities in the contract, and that all policy conditions are clearly revealed to the Proposer.

SECTION III

INSURANCE IN INDIA
– The Opportunities and Challenges

Chapters 7 to 10 take the reader onward from the level of theory to that of actual business performance.

How do you judge business results?

Usually, at least in the populist view, growth of Gross Revenues is considered to be the vital measurement of economic development.

In reality there are several other factors which are useful measurements of a business's growth or the lack of it. By focusing on any one parameter, and not giving adequate consideration to other significant indicators, we can get a skewed picture, with conflicting views about the health and progress of the enterprise. While some experts, basing their view primarily on growth of business volumes, would declare that the industry has flourished, others choosing to give primary importance to some other parameter could say with equal conviction that the growth has been 'slow,' even 'patchy.' In reality, there are several dimensions to the business performance of an enterprise, and each must be appropriately evaluated while forming an opinion on the subject.

In this Section, first the conceptual framework for judging 'insurance' business results is developed, and then the framework is used to analyse the actual performance of the Life and General Insurance Industry in the decade following liberalization in 2001. This is a hardcore, research based analysis founded on authentic data compiled from sources in the public domain. A short reference to the historical experience of the previous era of 'nationalized' business operations is provided to complete the picture and deepen the perspective.

CHAPTER 7
Perspectives on Change in the Insurance Industry

Perspectives on Change; From Nationalization to Liberalization; Liberalization and the New Era

From Nationalization to Liberalization

The Life Insurance Industry was nationalized by the Government of India in 1956, on the 19th of January, through an Ordinance. The Life Insurance Corporation came into existence in the same year. The LIC absorbed 154 Indian, 16 non-Indian insurers as also 75 provident societies—245 Indian and foreign insurers in all.

The General Insurance Industry was nationalized in 1972 through the General Insurance Business (Nationalisation) Act. With effect from 1st January, 1973, 107 insurers were amalgamated and grouped into four companies, namely National Insurance Company Ltd., New India Assurance Company Ltd., Oriental Insurance Company Ltd and United India Insurance Company Ltd.

The nationalized monopolies lasted till the end of the 1990s, and then the Insurance industry was reopened to the private sector in 2000. The wheel it seemed had turned full circle. It started turning from a stage of open competition with private participation, the condition of Life Insurance till 1956, and for General Insurance business till 1972. This was followed by a period of steady consolidation as a Government Monopoly, which later on degenerated into a state of bureaucratic lethargy that was bedevilled by red-tape, labour union obstructionism and missed opportunities. By the middle of the 1990s even the Government of India had come to realize that the socialist inspired experiment to create a 'mixed' economy had failed, and the economy had to be liberalized.

Liberalization and reforms came to the Insurance sector a little slowly. By the end of 1999 the Insurance Regulatory and Development Authority of India (IRDAI) was constituted as a Regulatory body to regulate and develop the insurance industry. Private Enterprises, equity participation by foreign investors, and open competition had returned to the insurance industry.

Prior to nationalization of the Life Industry in 1956, it was beset with several problems. There was intense, sometimes unhealthy, competition between the numerous companies. Business practices were not always fair and above board. Many Companies had failed to act as 'Trustees' of the premium funds managed by them, something which is integral to the very concept of insurance, but acted as owners for whom profits and business considerations were paramount considerations.[8] Product distribution was largely confined to the urban population and most companies only targeted the middle and upper classes. The overall health and financial stability of the life insurance industry was in a questionable state.[9] The 'History of Insurance' section of the website of the Insurance Regulatory and Development Authority of India (IRDAI) states that nationalization was the outcome of a situation where "…there were a large number of insurance companies and the level of competition was high. There were also allegations of unfair trade practices. The Government of India, therefore, decided to nationalize insurance business."[10] The nationalization of the General Insurance Business had been occasioned by circumstances where the business was almost exclusively urban centric, catering to the requirements of industry without addressing the other needs of society, especially the rural population.

In 1993 the Government of India set up the R.N. Malhotra Committee to propose recommendations for reforms in the Insurance Sector. The economy was being liberalized by a reformist government and the financial services sector had to undergo complementary structural changes. There were other reasons also. The nationalized insurance companies had some significant achievements to their credit, but their monopolistic and bureaucratic style of functioning had resulted in uneven and patchy development of the sector which had finally begun to stall and stagnate. On the plus side, LIC had spread the culture of insurance and savings beyond the urban middle class to rural locations, and along with the four General Insurance Companies it had vastly expanded the network of offices and intermediaries.[11] The Product portfolio has also grown.

On the flip side, there were some glaring negatives. The nationalized companies were afflicted by huge operational and structural inefficiencies, managerial atrophy, deficiency in service delivery to customers, and a lack of willingness, ability and agility to adapt to changing conditions in the marketplace.

The Government of India finally came around to the decision that the socialistic 'command' economy had served its purpose, and the changing times made it necessary to liberalize the economy. The liberalization of financial services and the insurance sector was a logical conclusion to the same process.[12] However, the process also created certain **expectations**, or perceived **opportunities**. It was believed that liberalization would result in:

Market Expansion: Spread insurance cover wider among the population

Service Delivery Enhancement: Improve the service levels and align them to global standards

Customer Choice: Provide the customer greater options for products and service providers

Operational Efficiency: Increase the operational efficiency of insurance companies leading to greater profitability in business and also delivering better products at lower prices to customers.

Resource Mobilization: Provide large resources for infrastructure development[13]

This brief survey of developments has provided us with a conceptual platform that shall help us analyze the growth and development of the insurance sector after liberalization at the end of this chapter.

Liberalization and the New Era

'Growth' and 'development' are words which carry a 'feel good' flavour. We associate them with improvements and positive outcomes, yet they have different shades of meaning, or signify different dimensions. What do we mean when we speak of the growth of an enterprise? What does growth refer to? Size? Market Share? Business Efficiency and Profitability? Product Quality? Service Delivery? Customer Satisfaction?! Most often people mean 'size' or 'market share' when they speak of 'growth,' but ideally it is a combination of all these features.

Progress, or decline, in the context of business, must be measurable and only then can it lead us to meaningful, objective and acceptable conclusions. How will we measure the progress of the insurance enterprise in a way which is not one-dimensional but holistic? Clearly, we must use not only one perspective, or measure one single dimension, to articulate our understanding of the overall development and growth of the insurance industry. We must measure activity and results in different functional areas such as business size, strategic economic impact, profitability, to name a few.

We shall therefore now first turn to developing an understanding of these concepts and then shall proceed to apply the concepts to business results to acquire a holistic and nuanced perspective of the progress of the insurance industry.

CHAPTER 8

Measuring and Understanding Business Progress — Conceptual Tools

Measuring and Understanding Business Progress – Conceptual Tools, Business Volumes, Strategic Economic Role, Market Coverage, Business Efficiency, Customer Satisfaction

The liberalization of the Insurance Industry in India began in the year 2000. We shall analyze its progress since then in terms of the following parameters:

1. Business Volumes (Size)

2. Strategic Economic Role (Insurance Penetration & Insurance Density)

3. Market Coverage or Reach (Distribution Network)

4. Business Efficiency (Profitability)

5. Customer Satisfaction (Customer Grievance Redressal)

Business Volumes and Growth in 'Size'

The real progress of the insurance industry can be best understood if we examine both the growth in volumes and the change in Insurance Penetration and Density. Volume Growth is usually measured as the growth in gross revenues. The Life Insurance industry refers to its gross revenues as *"Premium in Force,"* and the General Insurance Industry calls it the *"Gross Written Premium."* Both terms refer to the 'Top line,' which is the first point of reference used by the Management to judge business operations. The second reference point, of course, is the **"Net Profit After Tax,"** also called the 'Bottom Line' as it reflects the real 'profitability.' Only good and rising revenues make profitability possible. Without a 'Top Line' there can be no 'Bottom Line.'

However, a more complete perspective of the economic significance of the insurance Industry is achieved by examining the 'Insurance Penetration' and 'Insurance Density.' After all, Insurance is a segment of the Financial Services Sector, which itself is a part of the National Economy. It is illustrative to check the ratio a 'part' bears to the whole to understand its relative significance.

Strategic Economic Role – Insurance Penetration and Insurance Density

Insurance Penetration is expressed as a ratio of the size of the total Insurance Premium written in a year to the GDP of the national economy. It tells us how big is the insurance sector as a slice out of the whole, national, economic cake. For example, in 1999, on the verge of liberalization, the highest penetration measured in the world was 16.54 for the Republic of South Africa. The United Kingdom measured 13.35, USA was at 8.55, and India recorded 1.93 (*combined for Life & Non-Life Insurance*). Close behind India were Mexico (1.68) and China (1.63).

Insurance Density is a measure of the per capita spending on insurance, measured in US Dollars. In 1999 the density recorded was $490.90 for South Africa, $3244.30 for United Kingdom, $2921.10 for USA, and India recorded $8.50. The value for Mexico was $84.60, and for China it was $13.30.[14]

Market Coverage or Reach (Distribution Network)

Since Insurance itself is grounded in the idea of 'spreading' of risk as widely as possible it is natural, and necessary, for an insurance company to strive for the widest possible 'reach' in business. It would try to achieve the maximum possible coverage of the market space. Expansion of 'reach' requires two things. Firstly, an Insurance Company must build a geographically widespread and well distributed network of offices so that it can distribute its products in different corners of the country. Secondly, it must build a strong, numerous and committed team of distributors or intermediaries. Presently, all over the world, and more so in India, the individual insurance Agent continues to be the backbone of insurance distribution. This is not to discount the growing importance of alternate channels such as Bancassurance (selling through Banks), Broking (selling through Brokers who represent many Insurers) and Internet Sales (direct Web-based sales by the Insurer), but only to stress that the market place continues to be dominated by traditional 'Agent' driven distribution. Both geographical spread and a well organized team are necessary to achieve a more rational and balanced business model.

Business Efficiency (Profitability)

No one would have any difficulty in admitting that a business organisation must function efficiently and profitably, for no organization can continue to exist if it continuously makes a loss. Since insurance is the business of providing 'compensation' for loss of business assets, Insurance Companies continuously face the difficult task of making a 'profit' in the face of a succession of loss making events.

It is a business characterized by high volumes and slim margins where profitability is the outcome of four main factors [1] Underwriting [2] Claims Management [3] Expenses of Management, and [4] Costs of Business Acquisition (Distribution). It is important to understand how each of these affects profit margins.

Underwriting is the activity of prudent selection and acceptance of those risks which are 'insurable.' Remember, an event which is bound to happen, a 'certainty,' is not insurable. At the same time, if the losses are likely to be severe or extremely frequent, then also a risk becomes unacceptable. At best, an insurance company may either charge a very high premium for accepting 'high risk' exposures, or, in addition to this, it may also share the risk with other insurers through re-insurance. Underwriters also have to take precautions against fraud. At the 'Underwriting' stage of the business cycle frauds consist of attempts to insure an exposure after a loss has already taken place, or misrepresentation of the facts or features of the risk to obtain favourable terms. Pricing, or the rate of premium charged, is the other very important function of underwriting. If the pricing is adequate the Insurer would accumulate a fund adequate for the payment of losses, management costs, leaving a small surplus as 'profit.' If the 'price' is high the 'surplus' grows but the product becomes unattractive for the customer. If the price is reduced the adequacy of the fund comes under pressure. Insurance in general, and in India in particular, is known to be a 'price sensitive' business, and Insurers constantly face the temptation to drive prices down to attract customers from competitors.

Claims Management mainly covers the activities of determination of admissibility of a claim, assessment of loss, and calculation of the amount payable. It also consists of actions undertaken for control of frauds. The occurrence of an accident gives unscrupulous individuals the chance to inflate losses. Unfortunately insurance frauds are more frequent and ingenious than people commonly believe. It is easy in such an environment to start with an attitude of caution but carry it further to a mindset of suspicion, or even beyond. It is equally easy to be too trusting, allowing dishonest elements to take advantage of situations. The Claims Manager has a difficult task of maintaining the balance between caution and trust, between rejection and acceptance of claim and counter-claim, between give and take.

Both prudent Underwriting and efficient Claims Management have a direct and immediate relationship with Profitability in insurance business operations. At the primary or first level it is gauged through the 'Incurred Claims Ratio.' The Incurred Claims Ratio is the ratio of a systematically calculated valuation of Claims Paid and Outstanding to the Net Premium Earned. In simple terms it is the ratio of the outgo through claims to the income earned by the business. This ratio tells us whether the core functions of the business were profitable or not.

Customer Satisfaction

Customer Satisfaction is the last of the five parameters we had postulated as representative of the progress, health and efficiency of an insurance business enterprise. A high level of customer satisfaction reflects the good health of the enterprise and assures it of a regular revenue stream in terms of high percentage of renewal premium.

If a large number of customers are satisfied with the service delivered then their continued loyalty shall result in 'repeat' business orders. Since Life insurance policies are issued for long terms, 'repeat' business takes the form of 'persistence' of policies where customers continue to keep their policies in force by paying renewal premium when it falls due. As General Insurance policies are invariably issued for a period of one year or less 'repeat' business takes the shape of 'renewal' of policies with the same insurer by customers. In both cases customer satisfaction directly affects the revenue of the enterprise. In addition, since customers act as 'influencers' for their social networks and business circle, their satisfaction or opinion also directs or diverts customer traffic to vendors.

Most often, Organisations measure satisfaction levels for their customers through the medium of Customer Surveys and Studies conducted by professional Consultants who base their findings on data and responses obtained from scientifically selected sample sets of customers. Their Reports provide valuable and unbiased insights, but are a little difficult to use for making comparisons between organizations. For one thing different Consultants use different methodologies and scales of measurement, and for another, the time frame and periodicity of the surveys also varies.

For studying the effect of 'Customer Satisfaction' as a variable we have therefore used data for customer grievances and complaints published in the public domain by the Regulator (IRDAI). In 2011 IRDAI implemented a unique, industry wide system for the management and resolution of Complaints. Till then Insurance Companies had declared and submitted data for customer complaints received by them. The quality and integrity of the data depended upon the individual organisation. Now onwards, any customer can record a complaint either with their Insurer or with the Regulator. At both ends the complaints can be lodged directly at the Web-based portals or through the Customer Service Call Centers of the Insurers. In terms of system architecture the individual databases are synchronized and replicated every day with the database of the Regulator. Complaints recorded at either end are updated, and a uniformly categorized, more transparent and comprehensive, record is now available in the public domain. A high level of 'grievances' or complaints from the customer indicate a low level of satisfaction with services delivered. In addition, this data also helps us examine the reasons, or sector of operations, which have led to dissatisfaction.

The story told by these five variables of the progress of the Life Insurance and General Insurance Industry is presented in the two chapters which follow.

CHAPTER 9

The Insurance Industry – Business Growth

Objectives of Liberalization; Assessment of Business Growth: Top-line Growth, Insurance Penetration and Density; Profitability; Life Insurance – The Growth Story; General Insurance – The Journey

The Government of India and the other stakeholders, the insurance companies, consumers, intermediaries and service professional had high expectations of the overall benefits that would result from 'Liberalization' of the industry in 2001. In addition to Financial Growth, it was hoped that the Industry would provide superior customer service, wider product choice and expanded employment opportunities.

In this chapter we shall track the 'Business Development' of the Industry with specific reference to Gross Revenue, Insurance Density, Insurance Penetration and Profitability. Our exploration of Distribution Networks and Customer Satisfaction shall be conducted in the next chapters through differentiated narratives of the 'Life' and 'General' businesses.

During the decade from 1990 to 1999 Insurance business had enjoyed steady growth. The 'Life' business had grown at an annual rate of 20%, and the GI Industry at 12%. In 1999 the total size of the combined market was estimated at $8 Billion a year.[15]

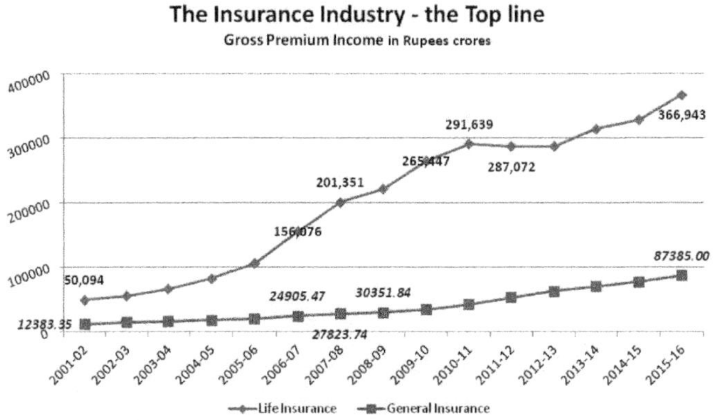

The Insurance Industry - the Top line
Gross Premium Income in Rupees crores

Figure 5: Growth of Business Revenue

Top Line Growth

The Life and General Insurance businesses experienced good growth of Gross Premium income during the period of 14 years from 2001–02 to 2015–16.

A glance at Figure 5 shows the Life business leaping ahead, while the 'General' business expanded, but at a more sedate pace.

The Premium Income, or 'Premium in Force' of the Life Insurance business grew from Rs.50,094 crores in 2001–02 to Rs.366,943 crores in 2015–16.

The Gross Written Premium of the General Insurance business went from Rs.12,383 crores to Rs. 87385 crores during the same period.

However, this picutre of surging growth begins to look more complex when we examine the year-on-year Growth Rates of both businesses during this period.

Figure 6 reveals that the growth rate of the 'Life' business followed a pattern of surging spikes and deep troughs. From a peak rate of 47.38% in 2006–07 to a rock bottom of − 1.57% in 2011–12, it went through some seemingly inexplicable fluctuations.

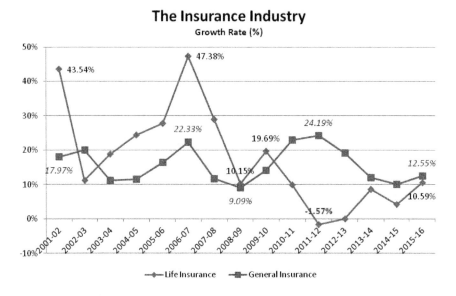

Figure 6: The Fluctuating Growth Rate of the Insurance Industry

The growth rate of the 'General' Business followed a more steady pattern. It never went below 9 per cent, and neither did it exceed the 25 per cent mark. We must add to our understanding of this growth story by examining the Insurance

Density for both the Life and General Insurance business as that will reveal another dimension of growth. The Insurance Density is the 'percapita' spending on insurance expressed in USD.

Insurance Density – a Rising Trend

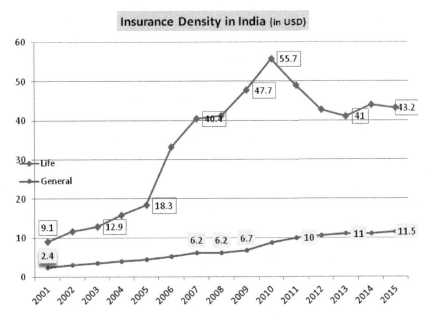

Figure 7: Insurance Density in India

The Insurance Density for both businesses, presented in Figure 7, shows a marked improvement from the base level of 2001. We can conclude that in 2015, when compared to 2001, the per capita purchase of insurance in India had grown substantially.

The Density for Life Insurance grew from $9.1 in 2001 to a peak of $55.7 in 2010, and then it declined to $43.2 in 2015 by when it was almost back to the level of 2007.

For General Insurance the Density grew at a much lower trajectory, From 2.4 in 2001 it grew to 11.5 in 2015. During a period of 3 years, from 2007–09 It remained almost flat before resuming its slow upward movement.

To complete our examination of the Topline growth we must examine the changes in Insurance Penetration.

Insurance Penetration – Peaks and Troughs

The Insurance Penetration ratio is an important measurement of the real status of the topline. It reveals the size of the business in relation to the GDP of the nation. Growth in Penetration signals that the Industry is growing in its significance or contribution to the national economy.

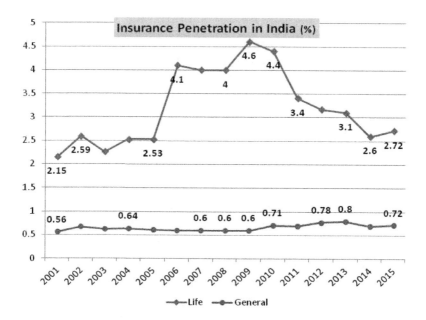

Figure 8: Insurance Penetration in India

The Insurance Penetration for Life Insurance grew from 2.15% in 2001 to 2.72% in 2015. During this span of 14 long years there was a period when from 2.53 in 2005, the Penetration peaked at 4.6 in 2009, and then precipitately declined, till by 2014 it was almost back to the level attained in 2002–05. The ground covered from 2005 to 2009 had been surrendered by 2015.

The Penetration for General Insurance changed from 0.56% in 2001 to 0.72% in 2015. During these 14 years it never surged like the ratio for Life Insurance, and though in some years it declined, it never fell precipitately either.

Our examination of the Industry's Topline, conducted from different prespectives, is now almost over. To add to our understanding of the real progress made by the Industry we must now examine its profitability.

Business Efficiency and Profitability – the 'Bottomline'

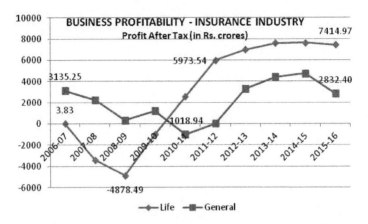

Figure 9: Profitability of the Insurance Industry

'Profit or Perish' is not just a catchy slogan, but the basic 'thumb rule' of survival for a business. It is the rationale for being in business. Both topline growth and a stable bottomline are necessary, and we must now examine the 'profitability' of the insurance industry.

'Profit After Tax' is the accepted final measure of profitability of an enterprise. Except for a strange dip in the initial stages, both the Life and General business achieved profitability for most of the period tracked by us. This dip bears further scrutiny and the subsequent improvement requires some credible explanation.

Life Insurance – The Growth Story

Life Insurance is known well as a long-term business, where a new enterprise breaks even after a period that could be eight or ten years long. Slowly the organization builds a large corpus of funds, which begins to yield profits over time. Till then the promoters have to sustain the business, and provide funds for projected liabilities, through capital infusion, as the business grows. In the initial years, before the corpus attains critical mass, claims could result in a 'loss' showing up in the annual accounts. After Liberalization new Private Companies set up operations and began to build on their foundations. LIC, however, was a stable business, a mammoth with solid foundations. From 2006 to 2010 it was the Private Sector which recorded huge losses, and when viewed at the 'industry' level, these losses offset the steady profits declared by LIC every year. This largely explains the dipping graph of net profits. Then, almost magically, the Industry began to show profits. What was behind the turnaround? Increasing Efficiency of Business

57

Operations? This could not be a reason as the Combined Ratio for Operating Expenses and Commission Expenses held steady between 16.55% to 18.60% during this period. The likely cause was windfall profits resulting from Surrender Charges or 'Lapse Profits' which are "booked by the insurer when the policyholder fails to pay renewal premium."

A report issued by Goldman Sachs, which was featured in an article in the Hindu's Business Line,[16] referred to the 2 year period of 2010–12, and drew attention to the phenomenon of some private Life Insurance Companies "reporting high profit growth for the past two years despite a slowdown in new premium income, due to the high proportion of lapse profits. But, what lay behind the high incidence of surrender charges, and why were ULIPs being surrendered?

The ULIPs were structured as investment products likely to deliver reasonable returns in the medium to long term, but were marketed as short term 'quick fixes' which would help customers get the benefit of rising stock markets. They sold like hot cakes till the economic recession of 2007, and for some more time after it set in. Everybody, the new Private Companies and LIC, placed great and growing emphasis on selling ULIPS, and they were a major contributor to the zooming top line growth. Till the markets seemed to be rising ULIPs remained attractive, and then their popularity declined. In 2010, IRDAI took strong steps to protect the interest of customers. It restructured ULIPS to cap the up-front charges, regulate distributor commissions, raise the payment periods and increase the ratio of Sum Insured to Annual Premium. As a result the ULIPs became unattractive for Agents and harder to sell as instant passports to financial gains. The Industry's Top line growth stuttered, Density and Penetration were impacted adversely. Customers unwilling or unhappy to 'invest' the heavy annual premium payable began to prematurely surrender ULIPs, and the amounts they had paid into the policy fund 'lapsed' to the Insurers and were appropriated as 'profits.'

This short analysis is meant to emphasize that the Life Insurance business depends on a long term effort at creating a stable business platform. Profitability is the end product of business efficiencies and widespread distribution of popular products that present a 'win-win' for all stakeholders. This is a business model largely followed by LIC which still commands about 70% of the market. Any deviations result in the kind of uneven spikes visible in Charts presenting Gross Premium, Density and Penetration.

General Insurance – the Journey

General Insurance is a business which is very different from Life Insurance. In a previous chapter the factors which drive the business have been analyzed in some detail. At this point it is enough to recap that the GI Topline is driven by 'Pricing' which is a function of Underwriting, and by an aggressive Distribution network. Till the end of 2006 the GI business functioned under a strict 'Tariff' regime under which pricing of products was strictly regulated. Everybody sold the same products at the same prices. This left 'Brand Equity' to act as the remaining differentiator between competitors. Brand Equity is nothing other than a reputation for 'reliability,' or 'trust' and the promise of 'service' in the event of a claim, but this only develops as a slow proces over time. In the interim period 'Branding and Marketing,' 'Advertising' and 'Packaging,' perception and expectation, acted as the differentiators. The new Private Insurers made an innovative beginning to establish themselves and the retail customer responded with enthusiasm. The 'Corporate' segment, historically well serviced by the PSU Insurers, was a little cautious to begin with, and it largely continued to patronize them. The GI Industry's revenues, or premium income, grew steadily and slowly the new companies started gaining market share.

Then IRDAI initiated the process of 'De-Tariffication' of the GI Industry. Beginning with 1st Jan 2007, the Insurers were allowed to discount or load existing fixed premium rates by 20%, and effective from 1st January 2008 total freedom to offer 'risk' based pricing was given to them. It was expected that prudent risk based pricing would benefit consumers. Those who had a good risk profile and history would be able to obtain lower premiums, and Insurers would realistically penalise those with adverse profiles. From 1st January, 2009 the Insurers were further allowed to offer customers variety in coverage, but not by changing the basis structure and terms of policies. Instead, they were allowed to devise and offer new 'additional' covers, also referred to as Add On covers, or 'Add-Ons' in short. They could also offer variety in coverage by varying Claim Deductibles and related Discounts.

The immediate effect of De-Tariffication was however quite different from what was expected. It led to a series of jerks and jolts as the industry adjusted to a new and more fierce level of competition. The freedom to charge 'risk based' rates led to a price war of great ferocity as everyone tried to lure customers with discounts that no one had earlier imagined were possible. Discounts spiraled and reached 50% of basic rates, then zoomed to even 90% for some products. In some cases, perhaps exceptional cases, it is reported they even went beyond.[17] The growth rate for gross business revenues (GWP) fell from 22.33% in 2006–07 to 11.72% in 2007–08 and stayed depressed for the next three years (see Figure 6). Beginning with 81.27% in 2007, the combined Incurred Claims Ratio for all lines of business deteriorated to 93.37% in 2010–11 and only recovered to the 2007 level in 2013–14.

The Incurred Claims Ratio is the ratio of Claims Incurred and expenses to Premium Earned. A high ratio leaves little margin for absorbing operating expenses, and costs of business acquisitions. As a result the GI Industry constantly turned in Underwriting Losses right through the period tracked above. In 2015–16 the Underwriting Loss Ratio was –19.73%. On 25th August, 2016, the Economic Times reported that Bajaj Allianz General Insurance Co. was the only Insurer out of 22, to declare an Underwriting Profit during 2015–16.[18]

The question could then be asked about how, in spite of an Underwriting Loss, the GI Industry managed to declare Net Profits. The explanation lies in the substantial income from investment earned by practically all Companies through effective deployment of the funds held by them. These allowed the GI Companies to offset underwriting losses with incomes from investments and declare net profits.

To summarize, as insurers came face to face with the declining profitability of their business portfolios, they realized the futility of a spiralling 'price' war for market share. After a 'free fall' that lasted for a few years prices again began to harden. By 2011–12 the market had begun to stabilize and the growth rate of Gross Premium income returned to pre 2007 level.

Our exploration of the Life and General Insurance business-scape shall now conclude with a brief examination of their Customer Service activites and Business Innovations in the next chapter.

CHAPTER 10

The Insurance Industry – Evolution and Development

Evolution and Development of the Business – looking beyond business growth: Development of Distribution Networks; Customer Service, Satisfaction and Complaints; Innovation in Product Features and Service Delivery; the uses of Technology

In the previous chapter we used changes in Revenue, Insurance Density, Insurance Penetration, and Profitability to analyze the growth and progress of the Insurance Industry. We will now carry the analysis forward by examining the evolution of Distribution Networks and the development of Customer Satisfaction. To conclude our analysis we will scrutinize some Process and Product Innovations through which the Industry has attempted to deliver superior value to customers.

Development of Distribution Networks

Life Insurance – Expansion of Networks

From 11 Companies operating through a network of 2199 Branch Offices in 2001, the network of the Life Insurance Industry underwent considerable growth.

The expansion peaked in 2010 with 12018 offices, belonging to 23 companies, and then the network began to contract as offices were closed down. The low point of this downswing was reached in 2013 with 10285 offices, followed by a slow, staggered recovery to 11071 offices in 2016 (see Figure 10).

It should be noted that Insurance Density and Penetration also hit their peaks in 2010 and then declined. The rapid expansion in the period up to 2010, and subsequent decline were largely on account of the operations of new Private Companies. All through these years the LIC slowly but continuously added to its Branch Office network.

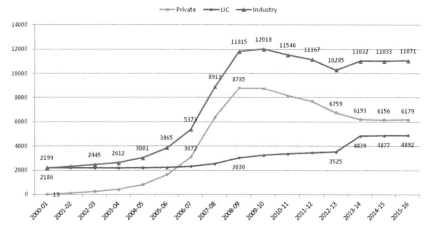

Figure 10: Life Insurance Office Network

Life Insurance – Hiring and Attrition of Agents

Reliable data for the strength of the Agency Team, the hiring and attrition, is available for the period 2007–16, and is presented in the next Chart (Figure 11). It graphically illustrates that the Life Industry vigorously recruited new Agents, sometimes hiring close to a million and never less than half a million new Agents. Unfortunately, the Industry also continuously lost a lot of the manpower that it had previously taken on board. From 2010–11 to 2015–16, the number of Agents who left the Industry exceeded the number of new recruits, except during 2013–14.

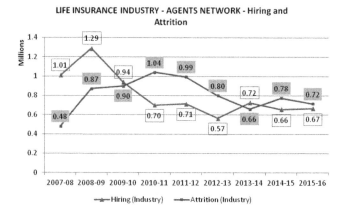

Figure 11: Life Insurance – Hiring & Attrition of Agents

62

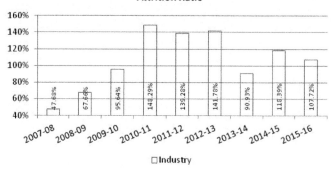

**LIFE INSURANCE AGENTS NETWORK - Attrition of Agents -
Attrition Ratio**

☐ Industry

Figure 12: Life Insurance Agents – Attrition Ratio

The Attrition Ratio represents the exits or termination of Agents as a percentage of the recruitments. At 47.68% in 2007–08 Attrition was already worryingly high, and it now climbed to alarming levels. In 2008–09 it climbed to 67.66%, and over the next seven years it exceeded the 100% mark during five, and was between 90–100% in the other two years.

The scale of the problem can be better grasped if we remember that most industries consider attrition levels of 20–30% to be intolerably high.

What is the significance of these two trends?

Firstly, recruitment of such large numbers, from selection to training, induction and deployment, requires a huge expenditure of an organization's resources. Attrition represents wastage of the resources spent. When Attrition takes place on the scale witnessed, then it represents wastage of valuable resources and loss of opportunity. Even more, it strongly indicates either failure of Strategy, Planning or Execution, possibly all three. It is a warning sign to rethink Strategy and Plans.

The expansion of Distribution Networks, both the opening of new Offices and hiring of Agents, is based on a specific and structured business plan. It involves heavy expenditure of resources and indicates commitment to development of the market in a particular area. Conversely, closure of Offices, especially those opened just a few years ago, and attrition of Agents, indicates a failure of strategy, planning or execution. In either case, if expansion of the network indicates buoyancy and positive intent, then contraction and attrition are bound to send negative signals to the market and stakeholders.

IRDAI's Annual Report for 2007–08 highlights the problem with the observation that "*One major concern that emerges from the data is the high percentage of turnover of agents. In 2007–08, while the total number of agents appointed is 10.07 lakhs, the number of agents terminated is as high as 4.80 lakhs. The high turnover is a huge drain on the financials of the insurers who spend lot of money and time on prospecting, appointing and training of these agents. The policies procured by these agents are rendered orphan on their termination and thereafter result often into lapsation due to lack of servicing support."[19]*

General Insurance – Expansion of Office Network

For the General Insurance Industry statistics are available only regarding Office Network, and data about hiring and attrition is not available in the public domain. It is therefore not possible to conduct the sort of analysis which was done for Life Insurance. However, the available data for Branch Office network of the GI industry is presented in the form of a Chart in Figure 13. Overall, there was a steady expansion of Branch Office network at the Industry level. However, there was a 'net' contraction of the Private Sector's network in 2011–12 and 2014–15. Such a contraction has the same implications for the General Insurance industry as it does for Life Insurance business. It signals the need to review strategy and plans.

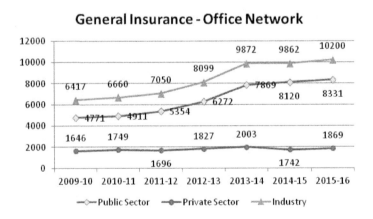

Figure 13: General Insurance Industry – Expansion of Office Network

Customer Satisfaction

Customer Satisfaction reflects the good health of the business and assures it of a regular revenue stream from satisfied customers. In Chapter 8 we had postulated it as the fifth significant indicator of the growth and development of the insurance industry. It is customary to analyze Customer Satisfaction on the basis of Customer Surveys and Reports produced by Management Consultants and Analysts. Here however, we shall use data on Customer Grievances now available in the public domain as a result of the Integrated Grievance Management System of IRDAI. This approach is based on the logic that Customer Satisfaction and Grievances are inversely correlated. Growing Customer satisfaction should be reflected in decreasing complaints, just as a rising trend for Complaints surely indicates declining Customer Satisfaction. Grievances and complaints also tell us why the customer is unhappy and what can be done to remedy it. A 'grievance' based analysis therefore has the advantage of highlighting areas in which the business can work to improve customer satisfaction.

The Chart of Grievances Reported for the Life Insurance Industry presented in Figure 14, graphically shows that the number of customer complaints sharply increased from 2011–12 to 2013–14. 'Unfair Business Practice' was the single largest category of complaints, and this rose sharply, though 'Proposal Servicing' related complaints, the second largest category showed a dramatic decline. Onwards from 2013–14 total complaints reported, as well as those under these two categories have declined, reflecting the improved delivery of services to customers. However, to restore perspective it must be stated that ever since 2012–13, 'Unfair Business Practice,' of which 'miss-selling' is a major sub set, is the reason for 1 out of every 2 complaints. This represents the single biggest point of concern and opportunity for improvement. Problems leading to Complaints related to 'Proposal Processing' and 'Policy Servicing,' the 2nd and 3rd largest categories, have been better sorted out, and Industry must now focus on restoring the confidence of a large number of complainants that they will be treated in a fair and equitable manner.

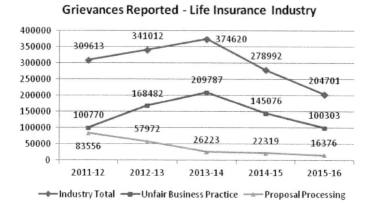

Figure 14: Life Insurance Industry – Customer Grievances Reported

The incidence of Grievances Reported for the General Insurance Industry from 2011 to 2016 is presented in the next Chart (Figure 15). Once again, the total complaints reported for the Industry have reduced substantially, indicating improved delivery of service, and higher level of customer satisfaction. However, the single greatest cause for concern is that the number of complaints related to 'Claims' has barely declined. If 'Claims' indeed provide the moment of truth in General Insurance, then this large and almost unchanging number of complaints highlights the area where efforts for improvement must now be focused.

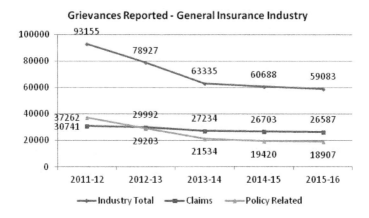

Figure 15: General Insurance Industry – Grievances Reported

Innovation, Evolution and Development

It is well accepted, and often repeated, that the objective of every business is the creation and delivery of value for its stakeholders. For the Owners of the Enterprise, the shareholders, value lies in 'business profits, the 'topline' and a healthy 'bottomline.' From the view-point of customers value lies in service delivery and customer satisfaction. For the nation value is measured in terms of the insurance density and penetration. Yet, there are some improvements and innovations which are not easily amenable to measurement in numbers. They can only be experienced and described. We now present some of the more significant innovations, practices and processes that have helped change for the better the customer's experience of service delivery by the industry.

Third Party Administration (Health Insurance)

Perhaps the most important of the innovations was the introduction of the system of Third Party Administrators (TPA) in Health Insurance Claims Administration, and the adoption of 'Cash-less' Settlements through a network of 'Preferred Garages' in Motor Insurance.

Till this point insurance claims had been settled as a rule on 'reimbursement' basis. The claimant first made the payment for the hospitalization or for the repairs to his motor vehicle, and then submitted his claim to the insurance company, which then paid out the claim. The entire process took considerable time and patience, and often a claimant only knew at the end the amount they would receive. It was a cumbersome and often uncomfortable 'pay now and collect at leisure' situation from the customer's point of view.

The TPA system was new for India though it was already well entrenched in the developed countries. It was new and different in style and method from the traditional, 'reimbursement' based approach to claims payment followed by insurance companies till then. A TPA was an independent organization that specialized in healthcare administration, and could work for several Insurers at the same time. It employed medical doctors and specialists in healthcare administration. It established a network of partner hospitals at which an insured could take treatment for contingencies covered by their insurance policy without making a deposit or upfront payment. The functioning of Third Party Administrators is regulated by IRDAI which lays down the regulations and rules under which they have to operate.

The TPA guaranteed payment to the Hospital for the specific amounts and contingencies covered by the insurance policy. They used modern methods of management and technology to deliver better decision making at higher speed. The hospital delivered the medical treatment to the patient, who only had to pay any small amounts not covered by his policy, and the hospital collected the balance from the TPA who handled the entire chain of operations on behalf of the insurance company.

This was not just health insurance providing a delivery of indemnity, but the extension of health 'care' to policyholders. Only claims for treatment taken at non-network hospitals were settled on a reimbursement basis, but these too were processed by the TPA. Not only was this system good for customers, it was also good for the Insurance companies, specially the new ones which did not have to create elaborate infrastructure or in-house expertise to process health insurance claims and could hire a TPA to deliver claim settlement services. It helped new insurers to quickly set up operations and go to market with their healthcare products. This system also made it possible for a policy holder to avail medical treatment without having to block and hold a large amount of funds in his Bank Account for this purpose. This added to the utility of the Health Insurance policy and boosted sales.

Preferred Garage Network (Motor Insurance)

Motor Insurance, in terms of revenue, is an even bigger business segment than health insurance. The 'system of Cashless Claim Settlement through Preferred Garage Network' functioned in a similar way as the TPA administered claims for treatment at Network Hospitals. The vehicle owner paid directly to the Garage that part of the repair bill which was not covered by the insurance policy, took delivery of his vehicle and drove away. The Insurance Company paid the claim settlement amount directly to the Garage. The claimant's cash flow was not affected by a claim.

Service Delivery – 'Service Anywhere' and 'Service Assurance'

Two more qualitative changes must be mentioned, and both were in good measure outcomes of the increasing use of technology. First, consider the idea of **'Service Anywhere.'** Before Liberalization, a customer could only approach his parent Branch Office to lodge a claim, to obtain a copy of his policy, or access any related service. At any other location it was virtually impossible to arrange service delivery. Computerization and Networking made it possible for a company to offer customers the facility of securing services from any office regardless of the point of purchase of their insurance policy. This did not happen in one giant step, but as a series of successive initiatives. However, it created a sea change in the mindset of the managers and their customers. Second, the idea of **'Service Level Commitments'** and **'Service Assurance'** grew out of the new management practices adopted by the private sector companies which were more 'process driven' than 'personality centric' in comparison to the PSU organisations. The requirement of adhering to a 'Turn-around-time' was central to process-oriented operations and TAT became a new addition to management speak and everyday vocabulary.

Leveraging Technology for Customer Communications, Interaction and Empowerment

Process improvements, innovative uses of technology helped Insurance companies not only to reduce operational costs but also to empower customers and provide them with a new range of experience. The growing use of technology and the internet brought companies closer to their customer and expanded service delivery.

Through **24/7 Call Centers**, accessed through a toll-free helpline, customers could intimate a claim, ask for product information, request for delivery of a duplicate policy, make changes to their contact details, or register a complaint. In fact, they could do almost everything which had previously required them to visit an office.

The **Company Website** became an accepted interface with customers. **Web Chat** facilities and email communications helped companies to deliver information and facilitate choice of product.

Personal Account Management and Self-help became available to customers who could create a personal account on the website of the Insurance Company and avail a variety of services. Web based transactions allowed them to renew policies. They could print payment receipts and policies using website delivered functionalities. In addition to a copy sent by post, customers began to receive copies through email as a routine.

Cell Phones also became another channel for connecting with customers. **'Alerts'** in the form of SMS were used to remind customers to renew expiring policies. 'Alerts' also kept them informed of the continuing processing of a claim from registration of claim, to appointment of a surveyor, completion of loss assessment to final payment.

Challenges – Today and the Future

The Insurance ecosphere in 2016 is very different from what it was in 2000. The business has come a long way from then, though none can deny that both Life and General Insurance are a 'work-in-progress' with much still to be done. So, what are the challenges before the Industry today, and what is the direction it must now take?

First, and foremost, lies the challenge of growth. The Industry has to find a model for sustainable and steady growth, and avoid the temptation to follow short-term methods which may deliver spectacular results in a few years only to then fade away.

Secondly, Networks for Product Distribution have to be built on strong foundations. This is a long-term endeavour, a marathon and not a sprint. Heavy Recruitment – High Attrition state of Agency Operations is extremely destructive and must be avoided at any cost. For the Life Insurance Industry this is an immediate necessity, but the General Insurance Companies must also ensure that they adopt more a long-term and visionary approach that excludes mindless discounting and price wars.

Thirdly, Team Building is vital for the effective management of the enterprise. Stability of the team of Managers is critical for this, and recruiting and retaining a team capable of building and leading a strong organization is of utmost importance.

Fourthly, it will be 'Service Delivery' which shall propel the industry forward, for insurance is a 'service' industry. This is not to discount the importance of other factors such as underwriting (product design and pricing) and operations (business process deployment), but to emphasize that it is 'Claims' which provides the proverbial 'moment of truth' in service delivery, and here excellence must be ensured. The cancer of 'miss-selling' must be eradicated. This requires the creation of a strong culture of 'service' in the organization.

Fifth, but very crucially, the business of insurance will take stronger roots when true awareness about its role as risk protection is created among people. Life Insurance is still viewed as an instrument for 'savings' and 'tax management' where it competes with other, often more profitable products. General Insurance is still regarded as a 'compulsion,' a option of 'last resort' and not as a pro-active device for risk management by a large cross section of customers. Dissemination of 'Product Awareness' should become a long-term objective for Insurers in the interests of their own future business success.

The Insurance Industry must transcend a transactional focus that limits the organization's vision to the Annual Balance Sheet, and pursue excellence as a strategy for delivering 'service' to customers. Only by creating value for its customers will it ensure delivery of value for the Enterprise and other stakeholders.

SECTION IV

INSURANCE PRODUCTS AND BUSINESS PROCESSES

Chapters 11 to 15 drill down into the Insurance Industry, and explore the different lines of business, the main products sold by Life Insurance and Non Life Insurance Companies. The emerging business segment of Micro Insurance and the challenges and opportunities before it are discussed.

Chapters 16 and 17 deal with the subject of 'Service Delivery.' They acquaint the reader with the process through which 'Policy Servicing' takes place and then discuss the core issue of "Claims Settlement.'

Chapter 18 is really not a part of any section, for it completes the picture by presenting the structure of the Insurance Market. It shows the relationship between the Parliament, the Market Regulator, Insurance Companies, Intermediaries, Loss Surveyors and Customers, and the various Law Courts and channels for resolution of Consumer Disputes.

CHAPTER 11

Types of Insurance – General Insurance Products – Marine Insurance

The MAR Policy; Marine Hull, Institute Time Clauses; Cargo Insurance,
Institute Cargo Clauses, ICC – A, B, C, Inland and Air Cargo,
Single Transit Policy, Open Policy, Open Cover

The General Insurance product portfolio is so large and complex that to make a comprehensive statement of all the features and nuances, of each product and its variants, is beyond the scope of this book. Here we shall confine ourselves, reluctantly, to a brief consideration of the main products and their significant features. The aim is to create a sense of the 'risk protection' offered by the product. Inevitably, some significant information, some important detail or the other, has been omitted, but a more comprehensive assessment must be left for another place and time.

The Insurance Act of 1938 forms the bedrock of Insurance Business in India. It provides the legal foundation and lays down the overall structure of the Insurance 'ecosystem.' Under the Act, General Insurance Business is classified into three types, 'Fire,' 'Marine' and 'Miscellaneous,'[20] and this classification has continued unchanged since then. Each of the three is considered a distinct 'class' of business.

Fire and Marine both soon developed homogenous sub-categories which came to be recognized as distinct 'lines' of business. With the passage of time, the number of Products under the 'Miscellaneous' category, and the volume of business, also grew so much that in practice distinct sub-categories have emerged and are recognized as valid classifications though they may find no mention in the Insurance Act. The most significant products, grouped by 'line' and 'class' of business have been presented in Tabular form below. Care has been taken to exclude brand specific product variants and include only generic products with the usage of accepted nomenclature.

Table 3: General Insurance – Products

Class	Sub-class (Line)	Product
Marine		
	Hull	MAR Policy with ITC Hulls Clause
	Cargo, Freight	MAR Policy with Clauses – ICC (A), (B), (C); Or Equivalent Clauses for Air and Inland Cargo, and Freight.
Fire		
	Material Damage	Standard Fire and Special Perils (SFSP) Policy
	Consequential Loss	Consequential Loss Insurance (CLI) Policy
Miscellaneous		
(Corporate Segment)		
	Property & Indemnity	Burglary Policy
		Money Policy
		Fidelity Guarantee Policy
		All Risks, Jewelers Block, Bankers Indemnity Policy
	Engineering	Machinery Breakdown Policy
		Erection All Risks Policy, Contractor's All Risk Policy
		Contractors Plant and Machinery Policy
		Boiler and Pressure Plant Policy
		Electronic Equipment Policy
	Liability	Workmen's Compensation Policy
		Public Liability Policy
		Product Liability Policy
		Directors and Officers Liability Policy
		Professional Indemnity Policy
	Aviation	Aviation Hull All Risks Policy, Aviation Personal Accident Policy, Loss of Licence Policy

(Retail Segment)		
	Motor	Liability Only Policy
		Own Damage Policy
		Motor Trade Policy
	Health	Hospitalization Policy
		Critical Illness Policy
	Personal Accident	Individual & Group Policy
	Travel	Overseas Travel Policy
		Travel Single-Trip and Multi-Trip Policy
	Package	Homeowner's Package Policy
		Shopkeeper's Package Policy
		Others – Office, Hospital, SME
(Government Segment)		
	Rural	Cattle, Livestock, Fisheries, Hut, other Rural Assets
	Mass Health and Personal Accident	Rashtra Swasthya Bima Yojna (RSBY)
		Pradhan Mantri Suraksha Bima Yojna (PMSBY)

Marine Insurance

Marine insurance has been described in the Insurance Act as contracts of insurance covering vessels of all description, the cargoes which are transported, and the freights on such cargo.

However, as it grew over time, Marine insurance business evolved into two universally recognized categories called

1. 'Marine Hull' which is the business of insurance of ships of all types, whether steam ships or sailing vessels, Ocean-going vessels or those plying on inland waterways, Passenger or Cargo Ships, Liners or Tramps or Chartered vessels, Petroleum Tankers or other specialized vessels for 'containerized' cargo. There is, also, no limitation on the size or 'tonnage' of the vessel.

2. 'Marine Cargo' which is for insurance of all types of cargo, from small parcels to large consignments, from 'Household Goods and Personal Effects' to Manufactured Goods, shipments of bulk commodities whether in cargo 'containers' or specially designed 'bulk carriers,' petroleum in tankers, etc.

At this point it is important to clarify that all cargo, whether transported over water by ships, over land by trucks, or by airplanes, is classified as Marine Insurance business. However, Marine Hull business is only concerned with the insurance of ships whether cargo vessels or liners. Trucks are insured under Motor insurance portfolio and the line of business for insurance of all Airplanes, passenger or cargo, is called 'Aviation Hull Insurance,' and both of these form part of the 'Miscellaneous' class of business.

The Marine (MAR) Insurance Policy

All contracts of marine insurance, whether for ships, cargo or freight, are made by issuing the Marine Insurance Policy, or MAR Policy as it is popularly referred to. However, this does not mean that the Marine class of business offers only one product to the customer. While the MAR policy form is used to record the details of the Policyholder, the property insured, premium paid and duration of insurance, 'Clauses' are attached to the policy to record the perils covered, contingencies excluded, warranties and conditions applicable. In this way, by combining it with different clauses, one policy form is utilized to provide a variety of products to address customer needs.

Marine Hull Insurance – the Institute Time Clauses

Hull insurance policies are mostly issued for a fixed duration, usually of one year. However, in rare cases, Hull policies can also be taken for a specific voyage. The specific terms and conditions of insurance are laid down in the 'Institute Time Clauses,' commonly referred to as "ITC – Hulls." *In Industryspeake the term 'Time Policy,' and 'Time Clause,' is used to refer to the insurance of Vessels, while the term 'Voyage' policy is used in association with insurance of Cargo.*

Coverage

A typical Hull insurance policy covers damage to the vessel by various perils such as (1) Fire, explosion (2) Earthquake volcanic eruption (4) Lightning (5) Stranding, sinking etc., Collision with other vessels (6) Piracy (7) Contact with aircraft, land conveyance, dock or harbour equipment (8) Crew Negligence (9) General Average Sacrifice. In addition, if the insured vessel collides with any other vessel, the policy covers 75% of the legal liabilities of the policy holder for damage to the other vessel, property on it or General Average settlement related to it. This is the core of the cover provided.

Ship owners invariably take a 'Protection and Indemnity' (P&I) cover for the remaining 25% of their liability that is not covered by the Time Policy. This P&I cover is not another 'insurance' policy sold by an Insurance company, but is a form of 'Mutual' assistance provided by a P&I Club. The P&I Club is a mutual insurance association formed by participating Ship owners who create a 'pool' by contributing funds from which payments are made for that portion which is not paid by a member's Hull policy.

Exclusions

The policy does not cover losses caused by (1) 'Atomic weapons,' 'Radioactive contamination' (2) Chemical or Biological or Electromagnetic weapons (3) Insolvency or financial default of the vessel's owners or operators (3) 'Deliberate' or wrongful acts of the owner or any person acting on their behalf (4) War (5) Strikes, Riots and Civil Commotion (6) Terrorism

Additional Coverage: On payment of extra premium the Insured can opt for coverage of (1) War (2) SRCC (3) Terrorism, though these are ordinarily excluded from the cover.

Marine Cargo Insurance and Clauses ICC (A), (B) & (C)

Marine Cargo insurance policies are traditionally called 'voyage' policies as they cover the cargo for the duration of its' 'voyage' or 'transit' from a specified place of origin to a specified destination. You will notice the contrast with a Hull policy which usually covers the ship for a specific duration of 'time.'

The Cargo policy offers a 'point-to-point' cover which starts when the loading of the cargo begins at the point of origin, continues during the voyage and any normal transhipment, and is effective till the consignment is delivered to the consignee. There are some qualifications and exceptions to this statement, but it is an accurate generalization which is true of the vast majority of shipments.

The specific perils covered vary depending upon whether the consignments are to be sent by (1) 'Sea' (2) 'Air' or are (3) 'Inland' cargo transported by Rail or Road. Quite obviously transits by Sea or Air include parts of the voyage where the cargo is transported by rail and or road, and a policy insuring Cargo transported by sea or air also covers the cargo. The policy records the perils covered by the attachment of specific clauses.

Coverage

Cargo transported by Sea can be covered by opting for Institute Cargo Clause (A), (B), or (C).

- ICC (C) which provides the most restricted insurance, offers cover against losses caused by (1) Fire, Explosion (2) Capsizing, Grounding, Stranding or Sinking of the carrying vessel (3) Collision (4) Discharge of Cargo at a 'Port of Distress' (5) Jettison of Cargo (6) General Average Sacrifice.

- ICC (B), in addition to the six perils mentioned above also covers losses due to (7) Earthquake, (8) Washing Overboard of Cargo (9) Entry of Sea, Lake or River water (10) Total Loss of Package during Loading or Unloading.

- ICC (A) offers the widest coverage, including all the perils covered under ICC B and C. It goes beyond both by offering cover for 'All Risks,' except those specifically recorded as excluded from the policy.

- Exclusions: The perils that are specifically excluded by all three Clauses, ICC A, B and C are (1) Insufficient Packing, (2) Delay (3) Inherent Vice (4) Willful Misconduct (5) Un-seaworthiness of Vessel (6) Nuclear Perils. Also excluded are (7) War and (8) Strikes, Riots, Civil Commotion and Terrorism, but both these, (7) and (8), can be covered on the payment of extra premium.

Air Cargo: The Institute Cargo Clause (Air) is applicable, and it offers cover against 'All Risks' other than those specifically excluded. The perils excluded are the same as those listed for the three Sea Cargo clauses mentioned above. However, only the excluded peril of 'Strikes, Riots and Civil Commotion (SRCC) and Terrorism can be added to the coverage on payment of extra premium. The policy cannot be extended to cover the peril of 'War.'

Inland Transit: Cargo dispatched by Rail and or Road for destinations within India is categorized as 'Inland Transit' Cargo. The coverage is available under the three options provided by Inland Transit Clause (A), (B) and (C).

- Inland Transit Clause (C) offers the most restricted and basic cover against loss caused by (1) Fire (2) Lightning.

- Inland Transit Clause (B) extends the coverage to (3) Breakage of Bridges (4) Collision, Overturning or Derailment of carrying vehicle, and on payment of Extra Premium can be extended to include (5) Theft, Pilferage and Non-Delivery.

- Inland Transit Clause (A) extends the coverage to (6) 'All Risks' other than those specifically excluded. By implication, Clause A covers everything that is covered under Clause B and C, and in additions covers all others which have not been mentioned as exclusions.

- Exclusions: All three Clauses exclude the same perils that are excluded under the Clauses meant to cover transits by Sea and Air, mentioned above. 'War' and 'Strikes, Riots, and Civil Commotion' are also excluded from the cover, but by payment of additional premium coverage can be extended to include SRCC only.

The Single Transit Policy: Cargo Insurance grew out of the need to provide insurance for individual consignments from their dispatch to delivery. The 'Single Transit' Policy fulfills this purpose. It covers a specific consignment during a particular voyage. However, purchasing such insurance involves a lot of administrative work, and a fresh negotiation of terms. The growth of industry and commerce created the demand for a stable arrangement which would provide insurance for multiple consignments and yet eliminate the tedious administrative paperwork and negotiations. This resulted in the development of the 'Annual Policy.'

The Annual Policy: As the name itself suggests, this type of policy is issued for an annual period. The terms, conditions, coverage, nature of cargo to be insured, the rate of premium are all, therefore, fixed for this period, both providing a stable insurance arrangement and reducing the administrative work for both Insurer and Insured. There are mainly two types of 'Annual' policy, (1) the 'Open Policy' and (2) the 'Open Cover,' each with several possible variations.

The Open Policy: The features of the Open Policy are (1) It is issued for an annual period, for which the terms and conditions are fixed (2) Multiple points-of-origin or the destinations can be chosen. However, one of these, the points-of-origin or the destinations, must be specified in the policy (3) The Sum insured is a value estimated to equal the total value of all consignments to be dispatched in this period (4) Premium for the full Sum Insured is collected in advance while issuing the policy (5) Declaration of Consignments to the Insurer is necessary. In its most basic form, the Open Policy requires the Insured to declare to the Insurer each consignment, with details of shipment, before it is dispatched. By special arrangement Insurers also allow submission or declaration of a consolidated statement of dispatches for a month or quarterly cycle. In some cases, to accommodate turnover high in value or volume a policy can also be issued on the basis of projected 'Annual Turnover,' thus removing the requirement for declaration of consignments (6) Accounting of Balance of Sum Insured under the policy is a continuous process.

Each consignment, dispatched and declared, is reduced from the Sum Insured, and the policy continues to be in force till a credit balance is available, after which it either lapses, or can be kept in force by payment of applicable additional premium.

The Open Cover: Has some features in common with the Open Policy, as, (1) It is also issued for an annual period for which the terms, conditions and rate of premium payable are specified (2) Multiple points-of-origin or the destinations can be chosen, but, one of these, the points-of-origin or the destinations, must be specified in the policy. However it differs in that (3) the Sum Insured is not specified (4) premium is not collected at the time the Open Cover document is issued by the Insurance Company and (5) Declaration of Consignments before dispatch is necessary so that the Insurer can collect required premium and issue an insurance policy for each shipment, as a result of which (6) Accounting of Balance of Sum Insured under the Open Cover is not required.

The 'Cover' is an 'agreement' and strictly speaking not an Insurance 'Policy.' The Insurance policy is a document issued after full premium and the applicable stamp duty has been paid to the Insurance Company. The Open Cover allows the 'Insured' to specifically declare to the Insurer each consignment at the time it is about to be dispatched, and to simultaneously pay premium on the settled terms. A specific policy is then issued for insurance of the consignment which has been declared.

We now conclude our survey of Marine Insurance products with the observation that while in the context of our objectives and constraints of space, an accurate outline has been drawn, yet, there is a vast amount of detail that remains to be explored by the interested reader. We must continue with a similar survey of 'Fire' Insurance.

CHAPTER 12
Types of Insurance – General Insurance Products – Fire Insurance

The Standard Fire and Special Perils Policy and Insurance of Material Damage; Consequential Loss Insurance

Fire insurance has been described in the Insurance Act as contracts of insurance against losses caused by fire or certain associated perils. The business is divided into two main types, or 'lines,' called (1) 'Material Damage' insurance and (2) 'Consequential Loss' insurance.

Material Damage – the Standard Fire and Special Perils Policy

This line of business is concerned with the insurance of property against physical destruction by the fire group of perils.

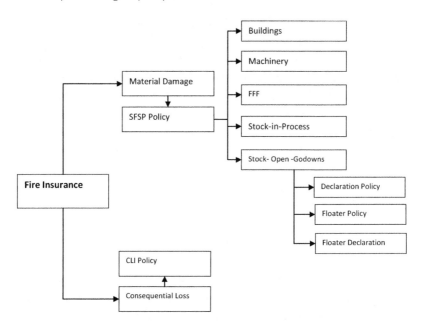

Figure 16: Fire Insurance Types of Policies

Types of Policy: The 'Standard Fire and Special Perils Policy,' or SFSP Policy, is the only product offered in this category, but through the option to select Additional Covers, also called 'Add-ons,' it can be customized to take care of all types of requirements.

The SFSP Policy can be issued to insure a variety of 'Exposures,' but which Industry insiders often refer to a 'risks,' ranging from Dwellings, Hotels and Restaurants, Shops and Commercial Establishments, Industrial and Manufacturing Enterprises, Utilities, Godowns and Open Storages. At any of these locations the assets which can be included under the policy are (1) Buildings (2) Plant and Msachinery (3) Furniture, Fixtures, Fittings, Merchandise, Personal Effects, etc. (4) Stock – in – Process (5) Stocks in Godowns or in Open Storage.

The SFSP Policy is meant to be usually issued for a Sum Insured, or value, which is treated as fixed for the duration of cover. However, to deal with situations where there is fluctuation in the quantity and value of stocks at multiple locations, customized variants can be issued such as (1) Declaration Policy, which specifies the maximum value for each location, but accepts a monthly declaration of actual values to derive the annual average value at risk (2) Floating Policy, which does not specify the Sum Insured for individual locations, but treats it as representing the cumulative value at risk for all location (3) Floater Declaration Policy, which combines the features of both Declaration and Floating policies. It does not specify the value per location while using monthly declarations to calculate Average value for each location. It must be stressed that these variants are available only for insurance of Stocks held in godowns or kept in open, and not for Stock-in-process.

Duration (Period of Insurance): This policy is usually issued for an annual period, but can also be issued for shorter durations, when it is commonly called a 'Short-period' policy. Some insurers also issue policies insuring Dwellings for longer durations up to ten years.

Sum Insured: The Sum Insured, or value for insurance, must be chosen by the Proposer. For Buildings, Machinery, Furniture Fixture and Fittings the basis of valuation can be 'Market Value' or 'Reinstatement Value,' but Stocks can only be insured for their 'Market Value.' Premium must be paid in full before the policy is issued, and the cover commences at a date or time of choice of Insured but after the premium has been paid in full.

Market Value can be easily understood as that value at which an asset of similar condition and age would be commonly bought or sold at a time prior to the occurrence of loss. In other words, the cost of a similar new asset should be reduced by depreciation for its age and condition.

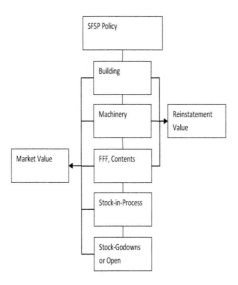

Figure 17: Fire Insurance – Basis for selection of Sum Insured – Market Value and Reinstatement Value

Reinstatement Value is the amount at which a new asset of the same type and capacity can be purchased or constructed as calculated post-loss on the date on which it occurred.

Coverage: The SFSP policy offers protection against twelve perils as a standard or fixed package, out of which the five most significant are

(1) Fire (2) Lightning (3) Explosion/Implosion (4) Riots, Strike, and Malicious Damage (5) Storm, tempest, tornado, typhoon, cyclone, hurricane, flood and inundation.

Additional Coverage: There are fifteen additional covers to choose from, the three most popular Add-ons are (1) Earthquake (Fire and Shock) (2) Terrorism Damage (3) Spontaneous combustion.

Exclusions: The Policy also excludes some perils, most noteworthy of which are (1) Burglary, housebreaking, theft (2) War (3) Nuclear Radiation or Explosion (4) Consequential losses such as Loss of Profits, Markets or Goodwill (5) Burning of insured property on the orders of a Public Authority

The SFSP policy, with its add-ons and variants, has stood the test of time in being able to provide a solution for all requirements of fire insurance against material damage.

Fire (Consequential Loss) Insurance

The SFSP policy offers protection against physical loss or destruction of property, and covers the expenses for repairing or replacing it. However, when such a loss occurs, then a Business Enterprise also suffers financial losses due to the interruption, retardation or cessation of its business processes.

The Fire (Consequential Loss) Insurance policy offers protection against financial losses resulting from a loss caused by Fire or other perils insured under a SFSP policy. The two policies go together, and the CLI policy is granted only if an SFSP policy is also taken at the same time. A loss under the CLI policy is payable only if it results from a loss for which liability has been admitted under the SFSP policy.

Coverage: The CLI policy covers (1) Loss of gross profit due to reduction in turnover or output (2) Increased cost of working which is the additional expenditure incurred to avoid or minimize the reduction in turnover. Here the Gross Profit signifies the sum of the Net Profit and Standing Charges, the Net Profit being the Net Trading Profit and the Standing Charges being those fixed expenses which are necessarily incurred and which do not decrease in proportion to a reduction in Turnover.

Additional Coverage: On payment of additional premium the policy can be extended to cover several losses, out of which noteworthy are loss due to (1) failure of Public supply of Electricity, Gas or Water supply (2) Material Damage loss at Supplier's premises (3) Material Damage Loss at Customer's premises

Exclusions: The policy excludes several types of losses, the most important of which are those arising out of (1) War and allied perils (2) Nuclear reactions and radiation (3) Loss of Goodwill and Loss of Market (4) Third Party Claims, Contractual Penalties and Fines (5) Material Damage Losses not admitted under the SFSP policy

Sum Insured: First, an Indemnity Period should be chosen. This is the period estimated to put the business back into its normal position, and could be any period from 6 months to 3 years. This is the period during which the financial loss is experienced. The Sum Insured chosen should be equal to the Gross Profit representing the Indemnity Period Chosen. So, if an Indemnity Period of one year is chosen, then the Sum Insured should be equal to the Gross Profit for One year. The Sum should be adjusted to account for estimated Increased Cost of Working.

In conclusion it must be stressed that both the SFSP Policy and the CLI Policy offer sufficient options to provide adequate solutions for all insurance requirements.

CHAPTER 13
Types of Insurance – General Insurance Products – Miscellaneous Insurance

Retail Business Segment

> *Motor Insurance –* • *'Liability Only' Policy* • *'Own Damage' Policy* • *Motor Trade Policy*
>
> *Health Insurance –* • *Hospitalization Policy* • *Critical Illness Policy*
>
> *Personal Accident Insurance; Travel Insurance; Package Policies*

Corporate Business Segment

> *Property & Indemnity Insurance –* • *Burglary* • *Money* • *Fidelity Guarantee* • *All Risks* • *Jewelers Insurance* • *Banker's Indemnity*
>
> *Liability Insurance –* • *Workmen's Compensation* • *Public Liability* • *Product Liability* • *Directors' and Officers' Liability* • *Professional Indemnity*
>
> *Engineering Insurance –* • *Machinery Breakdown* • *Electronic Equipment Insurance* • *Erection All Risks* • *Contractor's All Risks* • *Contractor's Plant & Machinery* • *Boiler and Pressure Plant*

Government Business Segment

> • *Cattle & Livestock Insurance* • *Pradhan Mantri Suraksha Bima (PMSBY) Yojna*

Miscellaneous Insurance

The Insurance Act defines 'Miscellaneous' insurance business, in the style of a residual category, as consisting of all business other than contracts classified as 'Fire,' 'Marine' or 'Life' Insurance business. The 'Miscellaneous' portfolio has grown with time and now consists of a vast variety of products which are organized in several distinct and well recognized lines of business. It is difficult to say which of these is the most important, but certainly some of them are bigger than others in terms of business volumes, some have greater visibility and customer recall because of their utility, yet others because of their strategic role in economic and industrial activity. The chart presented in Figure 18 is a diagrammatic representation of the Miscellaneous Portfolio and its various categories. The segmentation of the portfolio into 'Retail,' 'Corporate' and 'Government' business is one way of viewing Miscellaneous business.

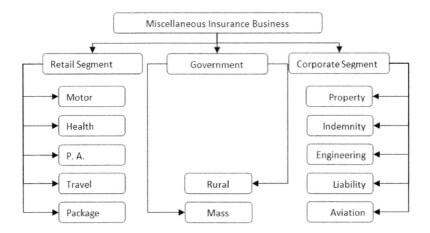

Figure 18: Miscellaneous Insurance – Lines of Business

Different classifications can be made, but this choice is based on the rationale that products listed under a segment are predominantly purchased by customers who belong to it. If the main business drivers, and the transactional sales and service style of a product line resemble that associated with a particular segment, then classifying the product under that segment is logical even though a significant share of business may also be contributed by some other segment. For example, Motor Insurance is transacted in the manner of retail products, the business numbers mostly come from the Retail segment. Yet, large numbers are also contributed by the Corporate segment. When it comes to business volumes this may be less true for Health Insurance, but the 'flavour' of the business is predominantly 'retail.'

All Miscellaneous Insurance Policies are usually issued for the duration of one year, but can be issued for shorter periods. The noteworthy exception to this practice is Engineering Insurance policies, which we shall discuss in due course.

Motor Insurance

Motor Insurance is arguably the most widely known type of insurance, perhaps because so many people either own or drive some sort of motor vehicle, and it is a legal requirement that each vehicle must be insured. There are three types of Motor policies, (1) the 'Liability Only' policy (2) the 'Own Damage' Policy and (3) the Motor 'Trade' Policy.

The **'Liability Only'** policy offers the basic insurance protection required while driving a vehicle on the road.

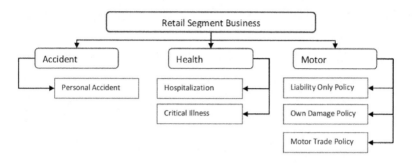

Figure 19: Retail Segment – Lines of Business and Products

Coverage: It provides the policyholder protection against 'Legal' Liability arising from an accident involving the Insured Vehicle for (1) Bodily Injuries to 'Third Party' (2) Damage to property of a Third Party (3) Bodily injuries to Passengers travelling in Public Service Vehicles. Personal Accident Cover for Owners who also drive their vehicles is mandatorily provided for specified amounts. The limit of cover for Legal Liability is defined. For bodily injury, the policy offers 'unlimited' liability irrespective of the type of vehicle. Liability for damage to property of third parties is limited to (1) Rs. 1.00 lac for Two-wheelers (2) Rs. 7.50 lac for Private Cars (3) Rs. 7.50 lac for all Commercial Vehicles.

Duration: The policy must compulsorily be issued for an Annual period, and cannot be issued for a shorter period.

The **'Own Damage'** policy is the one which customers mostly buy.

Coverage: In addition to the Legal Liabilities insured under the 'Liability Only' policy, it offers compensation for damage to the Motor Vehicle by a very wide range of eventualities, or 'perils,' such as (1) Accidental External Means, e.g. collisions (2) Burglary and Theft (3) Malicious Act (4) Fire, lightening, explosion, self-ignition (5) Flood, Storm and allied perils (6) Earthquake (7) Landslide (8) Riots and Strikes (9)Terrorist Activity (10) While in transit by Rail, Road, Air or Inland waterway, or elevator.

Exclusions: Compensation under the policy is not payable if the vehicle is driven by (1) Unlicenced Driver (2) Driver who is under the influence of alcohol or drugs, or the loss is due to (3) Electrical of Mechanical Breakdown (4) Wear and Tear (5) War (6) Nuclear perils (7) Contractual Liability.

Additional Coverage: Option is available to cover (1) Accessories (2) Electrical and Electronic additionally fitted to the vehicle (3) Wider Legal Liability for Drivers and Workmen (4) Personal Accident for Passengers. Many Insurance Companies also offer an option called 'Nil Depreciation' to remove deduction for depreciation from claims for partial losses or 'repair' claims.

Sum Insured: The value for which the vehicle should be insured, the Sum Insured, is called the **Insured's Declared Value (IDV).** For vehicles up to five years old the IDV is calculated by deducting depreciation on a fixed scale from the cost of a new vehicle of similar make and model. For vehicles more than five years old or for obsolete models, the IDV is a value determined by mutual consent between Insurer and policyholder. The IDV once recorded in the policy remains fixed for its entire duration.

Claims Compensation: In case of theft of the vehicle or its total loss, the Insured is compensated with payment of the full amount of IDV. For partial losses, or 'repair' claims the Insured receives the cost of parts and labour after deduction for depreciation based on a fixed schedule of rates which is mentioned in the policy. From the Amount of Compensation calculated a fixed amount termed **'Excess'** or **'Compulsory Deductible'** is deducted before the net amount is paid as claim.

Additional Features: The policy offers a 'No Claim' Discount if the vehicle has an accident free history and no claims have been made on the previous policies. The Insured can also avail of the option to have a **'Voluntary Deductible'** imposed in addition to the Compulsory deductible on claims and thus receive a further discount in premium payable.

Health Insurance

Health Insurance is of two types (1) Hospitalization Insurance and (2) Critical Illness Insurance.

Hospitalization Insurance

Hospitalization Insurance was started about three decades ago, in 1986, as a policy for individuals with the name **'Mediclaim,'** which has now become the generic name for this type of policy.

Coverage: It offers compensation for costs of (1) 'Hospitalization' (2) 'Domestic Hospitalization' where treatment in a hospital is not possible (3) 'Day Care' treatment for specified procedures, taking less than a day, that have to performed under supervision at a medical facility (4) Pre and Post Hospitalization treatment. Any treatment falling under one of these four classifications is covered.

Exclusions: The policy specifically excludes some conditions and diseases, most significant of which are (1) Pre-existing disease (2) AIDS (3) Naturopathy Treatment (4) Dental Treatment, unless requiring hospitalization (5) Plastic Surgery unless required as a result of some accident or illness (6) Specified Diseases during the first year of Insurance, with some Insurers varying this period of restriction, also called 'Waiting Period,' from a duration of 1 month, 3 months, or even over a year.

Eligibility Criteria and Sum Insured: The policy can be taken by, or for, (1) Individuals (2) Families (3) Groups. Different Insurance Companies have place varying restriction for the Minimum and Maximum age for taking the policy, but generally allow coverage to extend beyond such maximum age, or allow even new born children to be insured along with parents. The 'Group' Policy can be purchased by Employers for their employees or recognized Organization for their members, and for these the terms and conditions are suitably customized by Insurers to accommodate wider requirements.

The choice for Sum Insured per individual varies from Rs.15,000/- to Rs. 5,00,000/- and more, with some Insurers even offering coverage up to Rs. 1,00,00,000/-. The premium payable depends upon the age of the Insured person and the Sum Insured.

Claim Payment: The usual mode of claim payment is reimbursement of Bills after the treatment has been completed. However, most Insurers also extend 'Cashless' settlement, at least up to a defined limit. Under this mode, if treatment is taken a 'network' facility, that is, a hospital with which the Insurer has a contractual arrangement, then the Insurer offers to settle the Bill directly with the hospital without the Insured having to first pay them and then claim reimbursement.

Critical Illness Insurance

The Critical Illness policy offers compensation if the Insured person is diagnosed to be suffering from any one of the major diseases listed as 'Critical Illnesses' by it. Most policies cover between ten to twenty critical illnesses, a sample of which are (1) Cancer (2) Transplant of Major Organ or Bone Marrow (3) Multiple Sclerosis (4) Third degree Burns (5) Aorta graft surgery (6) Open Heart Replacement or Repair of Valves (7) Coma (8) Quadriplegia (9) Total Blindness (10) Kidney Failure.

The policy is sold to individuals, and is not sold to groups. Different Insurance companies have varying restrictions for minimum and maximum age for 'entry,' or original purchase of insurance, but once purchased, a policy can be renewed during the entire lifetime of a policyholder.

The compensation is paid out as a 'lump sum' if the Insured person lives beyond the "Survival period" mentioned in the policy. Usually the survival period is around 30 days from the date of first diagnosis or treatment, but can stretch up to sixty days under some policy variants. The compensation is meant to be payment of a 'benefit' and not a 'reimbursement' of actual expenses incurred.

Exclusions under the policy are made for (1) Pre-existing illnesses (2) Critical Illnesses contracted or evidenced within three months of policy inception (3) Illnesses resulting from use of alcohol, smoking, tobacco or drug abuse (4) Treatment for a Congenital disease, and others that are specifically listed.

The Critical Illness policy can be purchased as a 'stand alone' product, but is positioned as a buffer to the Hospitalization insurance policy.

Personal Accident Insurance

The Personal Accident Insurance policy can be purchased for individuals and also for groups. It covers persons between the age of five years to seventy years, providing structured compensation against Death, Permanent Total Disablement (PTD) or specified degrees of Permanent Disablement arising from an accident. An option to cover Temporary Total Disablement (TTD) is also available.

The policy can be purchased for any value, but Insurers like to link Sum Insured to a person's earnings from gainful employment. Usually cover is granted for seventy to hundred times of a person's monthly earnings. The premium depends on the type of cover chosen and the classification of Insured's occupation as more or less hazardous.

The Compensation offered is (1) 100% of Sum Insured for Death (2) 100% of SI for Permanent Total Disablement, or loss of any 2 limbs, hands or legs (3) 50% of SI for Permanent Partial Disablement (PPD), or loss of any one limb (4) between 1% to 50% of SI for specified permanent disablements (5) 1% of SI per week for Temporary Total Disablement. Along with Temporary Total Disablement, Medical expenses for a limited amount can also be covered. The policy only excludes events related to pregnancy, war, nuclear hazards, actions under the influence of intoxicants, and criminal acts.

The PA policy is an uncomplicated insurance product that offers compensation in the form of a benefit that is payable once the contingency has occurred, and is not an indemnity or reimbursement of actual expenses.

Travel Insurance

Travel insurance originated with the objective of providing assistance and compensation to Indian citizens travelling out of India to foreign countries for perils and losses they may face while abroad. The product, designed and marketed by the four PSU Insurers, covered specified contingencies

1. Medical Exigencies (a) Hospitalization due to sickness or accident (b) emergency dental treatment (c) evacuation to the nearest medical facility, or if required (d) Evacuation to medical facility in India (e) Repatriation of mortal remains to India, in the event of death

2. Personal Accident resulting in (a) Death (b) Permanent total Disablement (c) Loss of two eyes, or any two limbs, or one eye and one limb

3. Loss of Checked-In Baggage

4. Delay of Checked-In Baggage beyond twelve hours

5. Loss of Passport, leading to costs for issue of a duplicate Passport or Emergency Travel Documents

6. Personal Liability incurred towards Third Parties for personal injuries and property damage

The payment of compensation, with full decision making authority, under the policy was delegated to Authorized Agents who were located abroad and positioned to ensure on-location delivery of service.

The most attractive component of this policy was the coverage of medical contingencies. Indeed, the policy was named 'Overseas Medical Policy' or 'OMP.' To this basic configuration Private Sector Insurers have added some new features and a few tweaks to create a differentiated product. Some of the additional features are more like an amplification or extension of the original features, while others are a new dimension to the risks now faced by travelers. We may now look at some of these features.

- The 'Daily Hospitalization Allowance' compensates for small expenses that are incurred during a person's hospitalization but not included in formal Bill for Hospital expenses.

- 'Compassionate Visit' benefit covers the to-fro ticket of one person from Insured's family who may have to visit him during emergency hospitalization and convalescence.

- The 'Financial Emergency Allowance provides immediate cash liquidity to a person whose wallet is stolen, and who now does not have cash and, or, credit cards.

- The 'Trip Delay' and 'Trip Cancellation' features provide for the extra expenses incurred for alternative accommodation and onward travel arrangements.

- The 'Missed Connection' benefit provides for compensation of similar expenses.

- The 'Home Burglary Insurance' benefit covers the Furniture, Fixture, Fittings and personal effects of the policyholder at his home in India against Burglary and Theft during the period of his visit abroad.

Many Insurers have also developed special variants of the Travel policy for special segments such as Students travelling abroad for higher studies, or Company employees and Businessmen going abroad in connection with their employment or business.

Thus while for the leisure traveler there is a product which covers a single visit, for business travelers there is also a 'Multi-Trip' policy.

Package Policies

The 'Homeowner's Package Policy' and the 'Shopkeeper's Package Policy' were designed by the PSU Insurers to provide customers with a single product that offered multiple options covering all their possible requirements for insurance cover. Prior to this, a person wishing to ensure comprehensive protection for their assets had to go through repetitive and often tedious paperwork and obtain at least three or even five or six insurance policies. The Package policies changed that and made it possible to select desired options and take one single policy for all requirements. These two policies have provided a template which has been used by the Private Sector players to create variants like an 'Office' Package policy or an 'Industry' Package policy. However, essentially the idea and design remains the same. We shall therefore confine ourselves to discussing these two policies.

The **'Homeowner's Package Policy'** and the **'Shopkeeper's Package Policy,'** both, consist of ten or more 'sections.' Each Section offers cover against a particular group of perils. The configuration of cover under each section is fixed, and the perils covered and excluded, are not open to change by addition or deletion. However, the coverage is extensive, and would usually have been available only under a full-fledged 'stand alone' policy. The first section of both policies covers 'Fire' and other perils from the fire group such as Riot and Strike, Malicious Damage, Flood Storm losses, Earthquake damage, Terrorism damage, and this section is 'compulsory' or 'mandatory.' The buyer can select a minimum of two out of the other sections.

The Sections of the Homeowner's Package Policy are (1) Fire, and allied perils (2) Burglary, Housebreaking and Theft (3) All Risks for Jewellery and Valuables (4) Plate Glass (5) Breakdown of Domestic Appliances (6) TV Set (7) Pedal Cycles (8) Baggage insurance (9) Personal Accident and (10) Public Liability.

The Sections under the Shopkeepers Policy are (1) Fire, and allied perils for Building and Contents (2) Burglary and Housebreaking (3) Money Insurance (4) Pedal Cycles (5) Plate Glass (6) Neon Sign or Glow Sign (7) Baggage insurance (8) Personal Accident (9) Fidelity Guarantee (10) Public Liability and (11) Loss of Profits.

The two policies are designed to offer options for the different requirements of a Homeowner and a Shopkeeper, but the similarities in concept and design are evident. The various Sections represent individual products most of which we are either going to examine as separate products, or which we have already examined. Hence we shall not expend effort at this point in discussing coverage under "Fire,' 'Burglary,' 'Money,' "Machinery Breakdown,' 'Personal Accident,' 'Fidelity Guarantee,' 'Public Liability' or 'Loss of Profits.' However, it would be appropriate to offer a brief explanation for:

Pedal Cycle Insurance: This covers pedal cycles against any unforeseen physical loss or damage. The usual types of losses experienced, and which are covered, are those by theft, fire, malicious act, terrorism, etc. Personal legal liabilities of the Insured to third parties are also covered.

Baggage Insurance: The personal baggage of the Insured, or their family members, for the specified value, is insured against theft during travel in India. Baggage lost while kept in a car is also covered provided the car's doors and windows are properly locked at that time. The cover does not extend to a situation where the baggage is being transported by a carrier under a contract of affreightment.

Pate Glass Insurance: This provides for compensation for breakage of Plate Glass or mirrors that are properly fixed, to supporting structure, framework or masonry. Glass which is not properly and securely fixed or mounted, and is in a movable condition, is not covered.

Neon Sign Insurance: Neon Signs are covered against loss by fire, storm and floods, earthquakes, riots and strikes, terrorist damage, theft and accidental external means.

Corporate Business Segment

Property and Indemnity Insurance Products

We shall review six policies under the 'Property and Indemnity' business category.

Burglary Insurance: This policy is a product of long standing, which was originally designed for commercial or industrial establishments, but was then extended to individual customers for domestic assets. It offers cover for contents and 'stocks' in any business against loss by 'Burglary & Housebreaking,' which are defined as theft by means of a forceful entry or exit from a premises, or the threat of use of Force against the Insured and his employees or representatives. It should be noted that the use or threat of use, of force is an essential part of the definition of 'Burglary.' Unless this condition is met, the loss, even if it is caused by theft, would not qualify as payable under the policy. Therefore, an ordinary theft, or one where a key was used to gain entry to or to exit from the premises would not be payable under the policy which also excludes all acts where the Insured or his employees or family members are an accomplice or accessory to the crime. However, when this policy is issued to individuals for covering domestic assets then the ordinary cover against Burglary and Housebreaking is extended to include ordinary theft committed without any element of force.

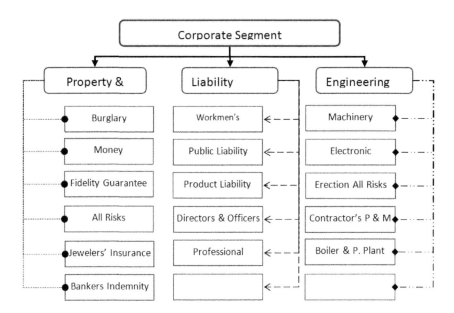

Figure 20: Corporate Segment – Lines of Business & Types of Products

Money Insurance: This policy is meant for coverage of the money belonging to a commercial establishment while (1) In transit from or to a Bank or specified Offices and Locations while it is in the custody of authorized representatives (2) In 'Safe' or any specialized storage facility for the overnight keeping of 'Money' after business hours (3) At Cash Counter, or 'Till,' during regular Business hours. 'Money' is defined to include Cash, Cheques, Bank Drafts, Treasury Notes, Postal Orders and stamps, and is covered against loss by Burglary, Theft, Robbery or any fortuitous cause. Loss caused by dishonesty or fraud of employees is excluded, but can be covered on payment of extra premium.

Fidelity Guarantee: This policy protects an Employer against financial loss caused by the dishonesty, or 'infidelity,' of an employee. Uniquely, not only does the policy cover losses due to act committed (1) During the period of insurance, but also (2) those committed during a period of uninterrupted service with the Insured but discovered within the policy period or within twelve months of its expiry, and (3) in case of the death, dismissal or retirement of an employee, if discovered within twelve months of the death, dismissal or retirement. The Policy records the limits of liability covered for each employee, either by individual names, or by designations and categories. The Employer is required to initiate suitable action, including launch of criminal proceedings against the Employee accused of infidelity or fraudulent act, and to suitable restrain or totally remove him from work to prevent any recurrence.

All Risks: The All Risks policy is meant for the coverage of the Jewelry, whether ornaments of gold, silver or other precious metals, curios, cameras, watches or other such valuable articles belonging to a person or his family. While most policies cover a property while at a specified location, this policy recognizes that Jewelry is most at risk when worn, and not just when it is stored, and therefore the policy covers articles without limitation to location. However, at insurance, each article is listed with a specific value which is expected to be based on the valuation certified by a qualified Jeweler. The cover is either against 'All Risks' other than those specifically excluded, or can be very extensive, stretching from Fire, Theft, Riot and Strike, Accident, and any 'Fortuitous Cause,' thus giving protection against any conceivable and legitimate contingency. However, the policy does specifically exclude damage by (1) Cleaning, repairing, restoration, wear and tear (2) Breakage, scratching or cracking of articles of glass or of fragile nature (3) Mechanical or Electrical Breakdown unless it is the result of accidental external means (4) Theft from a Car unless it is a fully enclosed 'Saloon' type of vehicle which is properly locked at the time of loss.

Jewelers Insurance: This policy is designed to provide insurance solutions for Jewelers with respect to their stock-in-trade and associated assets. It covers Ornaments, Plate and Bullion, gems, money (1) while at the Jewelers establishment against fire, burglary, robbery, riot and strike, and malicious damage (2) while in the custody of the Insured, partners, employees or goldsmiths and workers entrusted with it, against the perils mentioned above (3) during transit by Registered Post Parcel,

Air Freight or Angadias, and also covers (4) Furniture, Fixtures and Fittings of the Jeweller's establishment. The policy was only to be issued to Jewelers, whether Retails or Wholesale, but not to those primarily only manufacturing jewellery like goldsmiths or diamond cutters, or pawnbrokers or Angadias.

Bankers Indemnity: This is a package policy targeted at Banks. It covers all the Administrative offices, branches, sub offices and establishments of a Bank. The money and banking instruments are covered against contingencies such as (1) On Premises, against fire, riot and strike, malicious damage, burglary, robbery, hold-up (2) In Transit, if lost, stolen, mislaid, whether due to negligence or fraud of employees (3) by Forgery or alteration of Banking instruments by criminal acts whether of employees or others (4) while being sent by Registered Post Service, or, (5) while in the custody of registered appraisers of the bank.

Liability Insurance Products

Workmen's Compensation: If a workman is injured during the course of his employment then the Employer is legally liable to pay compensation to him for the injuries or disabilities, or to the legal heirs in case of death. This policy compensates an Employer for payment of compensation as required under provisions of (1) The Workmen's Compensation Act, 1923 (2) The Fatal Accidents Act, 1855, (3) Common Law. It also pays for any legal costs in case there is litigation contesting the claim. The policy covers not only the employees of the Insured but also workmen employed by a Contractor or sub-contractor, though for this additional premium may be charged.

Public Liability: This policy provides Organizations and Incorporated Companies cover against legal liability to pay damages to third parties as a consequence of death, injury or damage to property. The cost of litigation is also covered. Such 'civil' liabilities are said to arise when there is some alleged negligence on the part of the Insured leading to the third party suffering death, injury or damage to property. The policy can be extended to provide additional cover for liabilities arising out of events which may have themselves been the result of natural calamities like flood or earthquakes, or related to 'Pollution' traceable to the Insured, or linked to the transportation of hazardous material or effluents by the Insured. A unique feature is that the coverage is for a 'Retroactive Period.' This concept should be clearly understood. If a policy has been in force with the insurers for several years in the past, then a claim made under the current policy but for an event that occurred during the effective period of any of the past policies, called 'retroactive' period is held covered.

There are three variants of this policy , (1) Public Liability – Non Industrial Risks, for Offices, Hotels, Cinemas, Hospitals, Schools, etc (2) Public Liability – Industrial Risks, for Factories and Godowns (3) Public Liability Insurance Act 1991 policy, for owners, users or transporters of hazardous materials taken in compliance with the provisions of the Act.

Product Liability: Manufacturers of products, whether they are 'final' products for use, or form part of a product, are exposed to the contingency of being held legally liable to third parties who may suffer death, injury or property damage due to some manufacturing defect in the product, in the packaging or delivery, or the instruction about use. The policy covers legal costs also. The cover under the policy is effective for the Retroactive period.

Directors and Officers Liability: Any decision or action taken by a Director or Officer of a Company, whether individually in their official capacity or jointly with colleagues, even after full care is taken to comply with all laws, could have inadvertent consequences resulting in infringement of some law or regulation. This could result in prosecution, legal costs, and award by Courts of damages to third parties, all of which would be a loss to the Company. The possibility for such mishaps is increasing in a world that is integrating into one global marketplace, where even the laws in any two countries may not be the same, and a perfectly normal action in one country could be' non-compliant' in another.

The 'D & O' Liability policy provides compensation for Loss to the Organization due to (1) Mistaken Actions taken by Directors or Officers in their individual capacity (2) Wrongful Acts committed in official capacity (3) Legal Expenses associated with Legal Defense (4) Award by Law Courts of Legal Expenses of Shareholders proceeding against a Director or Officer. The policy excludes (1) all dishonest, fraudulent or malicious acts (2) Bodily Injury or Damage to Property of Third Party (3) Personal Guarantee (4) Libel and Slander (5) Pollution damage (6) Product Liabilities.

Professional Indemnity: This policy is meant to cover the legal liability of Professional persons for their 'Errors or Omissions' of action or advice while delivering professional services. Legal costs and expenses are also covered. The policy is effective for the 'retroactive' period. Only 'civil' liabilities are covered, and all 'criminal' liabilities are excluded. The policy can be taken by (1) Doctors and Medical Practitioners (2) Medical Establishments (3) Engineers, Architects and Interior Decorators (4) Lawyers (5) Chartered Accounts, Financial Accountants and Management Consultants.

Engineering Insurance Products

Of the six products that are classified under the Engineering Insurance category, perhaps Machinery Breakdown insurance is the oldest, and the one which most often comes to mind, though others are equally important in terms of their role in risk management.

Machinery Breakdown: Plant and Machinery is an integral part of all industrial and commercial operations. All types of machines can be insured under this policy against loss arising from accidental electrical and mechanical breakdown. Additional cover can be taken for the civil works, surrounding property of Insured and Third Party liabilities. The machinery must be insured for a value equal to cost of a new machine of the same type. The policy excludes losses caused by (1) faulty workmanship or materials (2) failure of lubrication (3) mal-functioning of safety devices (4) electrical short-circuiting (5) entry of a foreign body in a running machine.

Electronic Equipment: The Electronic Equipment Insurance (EEI) policy is designed to cover the entire range of electronic equipments, from those meant for domestic use to those for commercial and industrial use. It can be used to cover Computers, Television sets, Data Processing and Telecommunications equipment, Audio-Video Transmitting and Receiving Installations, Cinema, Sound Reproduction and Studio equipment, Medical equipments, Industrial Control and Supervisory units, and similar equipments. The cover is against sudden, unforeseen damage by accidental external means, except those specifically excluded. As such some of the significant perils and losses covered are Fire and allied perils, Flood and Earthquake damage, Riot and Strike, Malicious damage and Terrorism losses, Burglary and Theft, Short-circuiting and electrical fire, damage by falling objects, water, humidity, smoke and dust. The policy excludes losses by 'wear and tear,' loss to consumables and operating media, consequential losses, those which are the contractual responsibility of other parties, due to war or gross negligence.

Erection All Risks: This policy is designed to provide coverage during the 'project' stage. It insures Plant, Machinery, steel structures and associated civil work during the stage of construction-installation against accidental losses by any peril except those specifically excluded. It is therefore an 'all risks' type of cover as what is not covered is specifically mentioned, and everything else is covered during the stage of storage, erection, construction, testing and commissioning of the project.

The range of perils covered and losses usual experienced range from (1) Fire and allied perils (2) Riot and Strike, Malicious damage (3) Flood etc damages (4) Burglary (5) Landslide and subsidence, Collapse (6) Impact damage and due to foreign objects, and very significantly, (7) Faults in Erection and (8) Human Error. The cover can be further extended on payment of extra premium to include 'Liability to Third Parties' and perils such as Earthquake, Terrorism and Damage to Surrounding Property.

The policy specifically excludes losses caused by (1) Faulty design, defective material or bad workmanship (2) Manufacturing defects (3) Willful negligence (4) Wear and tear (5) Inventory losses (6) War (7) Nuclear hazards.

The insurance policy is issued for the full 'project period' which could be less or more than a year, starting from the time of arrival of the first consignment at project site, extending through period of storage, erection, testing and final commissioning of the insured project. Anyone who is the Owner, Contractor, Sub-contractor or a Financier of the project can take this policy. If the policy period extends beyond one year the premium can be paid in installments.

Contractors All Risks: This policy is meant for insurance of Civil Engineering projects, or those where the civil works form the predominant part and plant or machinery is a negligible component. This is in contrast with target segment of the Erection All Risks policy which is projects which are for erection of Plant and Machinery, and where civil works are only a necessary and associated component. In all other respects regarding features, coverage, exclusions and policy administration these two policies are similar.

Contractor's Plant and Machinery: Plant and Machinery belonging to a Contractor and used on-site for the construction or erection of a project is exposed to various hazards. This policy offers cover for such Plant and Machinery at the project site, while it is in use, at rest, being moved within the site or dismantled for maintenance and overhaul. The coverage is against all perils, risks and losses other than those specifically excluded. As such, the bouquet of coverage is much the same as that under the EAR and CAR policies reviewed above. In addition to the main exclusions under those policies, the CPM policy also excludes the damages related to (1) electrical and mechanical breakdown, lack of lubrication or coolant (2) movable parts such as bits, drills (3) wear and tear (4) while in transit between different locations. This policy is issued for an annual period.

Boiler and Pressure Plant: This is a less known but valuable coverage for Industrial Boilers, Pressure Vessels and steam pipes. These are covered against (1) Damage, excepting damage by fire, notably by Explosion or implosion (2) Damage, other than by fire, to surrounding property (3) Legal Liability to Third Parties for bodily injury and damage to property. The policy specifically excludes Fire and the allied perils covered under the Fire policy, as well as specific conditions connected to the operation of such equipment.

Government Business Segment

Both 'Rural Insurance' business and the 'Mass Health' segment have been classified under the category of 'Government' business, only for the reason that the main business driver for both has been government initiatives rather than the evolution or crystallization of 'demand' from consumers. Most products from these categories are also classified as 'Micro Insurance' which is discussed a little later in another chapter.

Rural Insurance witnessed extensive product development at the hands of the four Public Sector insurance companies during the period following nationalization of General Insurance business. They created a product for every conceivable rural asset from Cattle and other agricultural livestock, to fisheries, Poultry, Sericulture and Honeybees, down to Huts, Animal Driven Carts and Agricultural Pump sets. Attempts have also made to develop 'Mass' insurance products for insurance of 'persons.' At this place we shall briefly examine two products to acquire an overall perspective.

Cattle and Livestock Insurance: The standard policy insured individual Milch animals and Stud Bulls or Buffaloes for a Sum equal to their Market Value. These were covered against the contingency of Death or Permanent Total Disablement if resulting from accident, illness, surgical operation or due to Riot or Strikes. The full Sum Insured was payable in case of death, and 75% in case of PTD which was defined as the total inability to yield milk, or to calve, or to perform the purpose of acquisition declared at the time of insurance. The policy excluded the usual perils commonly excluded from General Insurance policies such as intentional injury, war or nuclear hazards.

Pradhan Mantri Suraksha Bima Yojna (PMSBY) Policy: This is an example of the mass 'Group' insurance product, for insurance of 'persons,' targeting both Rural and Urban buyers. The Scheme under which these policies are sold was launched in 2015. The scheme is to be administered and operated by the Banking sector. All Banks are required to offer to their Savings Bank Account holders, between the age of 18 to 70 years, the opportunity to voluntarily join the Scheme after paying premium which would be directly debited to their Bank Account. The Bank was free to choose any Insurance Company, whether Public Sector or Private Sector, as its partner for Insurance services. The enrollment was for an initial period from 1st June 2015 to 31st May 2016, and could be continued year-on-year after that for similar durations. The enrolled persons were granted a 'Personal Accident' cover for a Capital Sum Insured of Rs. 2.00 lac, which was payable in the event of Death or Permanent Total Disablement, i.e. loss of two eyes, or any two limbs, or one limb and one eye, as a result of any 'accident.' An amount of Rs. 1.00 lac was payable for the loss of one eye or of any one limb. The annual premium payable was Rupees Twelve only. This is an affordable product, with simple features, meant for the 'mass' market, being offered to a very wide customer segment through the extensive distribution network of the Banking sector. In its features and structure this policy has much in common with the 'Janata Personal Accident' Policy of 1980s vintage, which never sold well enough to attain popular recognition, but neither faded away with time, and still forms a part of the PSU product portfolio.

The demand and sales of policies like the JPA and the Cattle insurance policy was a byproduct of Government schemes for the economic development of rural India, which revolved around asset creation on the basis of finance provided through the Banking Sector. Insurance of these assets was necessary to protect the financial interest of the Banks, and that is what drove the demand. The story of this economic journey, its highpoints and troughs, with data and analysis, has been told elsewhere by scholars, and shall not be repeated here.

We shall now conclude this exploration of General Insurance products of which we examined a very significant cross section.

References

[1] "All about critical illness plans and how to choose one"; Tomorrow Makers; April 4, 2016; http://economictimes.indiatimes.com/your-money/all-about-critical-illness-plans-and-how-to-choose-one/tomorrowmakersshow/51810014.cms; extracted on 18.01.2017

[2] Bharati Axa Critical Illness Insurance; Extracted on 18.01.2017; https://www.bharti-axagi.co.in/critical-illness-insurance

[3] "Do you need a critical illness plan?"; Extracted on 18.01.2017; http://www.livemint.com/Money/htnUzjrnlOmLYr43Jc1v2M/Do-you-need-a-critical-illness-plan.html

[4] Money Insurance Policy, Bharti Axa General Insurance Co. Ltd; https://www.irda.gov.in/ADMINCMS/cms/Uploadedfiles/35.%20Money%20%20Policy%20Wordings.pdf; Extracted on 24.01.2017

[5] Money Insurance; Highlights; New India Assurance Co.; http://www.newindia.co.in/Content.aspx?pageid=58; Extracted 24.01.2017

[6] Fidelity Guarantee Insurance: Highlights; New India Assurance Co.; http://www.newindia.co.in/Content.aspx?pageid=10; Extracted on 24.01.2017

CHAPTER 14
Types of Insurance – Life Insurance Products

Lines of Business in Life Insurance; Life Insurance Products

Though the term 'line of business' is usually used in the field of Non-Life or General Insurance, we can use the same idea to separate Life Insurance into two distinct categories, one being Pensions and Annuities and Insurance being the other. Pension and Annuity products do not offer any risk cover while Life Insurance products do not provide any payments in the manner annuities do.

It is said that Annuities and Life Insurance work in 'opposite' ways. Life insurance requires a person to pay regular and small contributions (premiums) to the Insurer for a specified period towards the creation of 'capital,' a risk 'fund,' by the insurer, and on the occurrence of death, or after a specified period the Insurer pays back a specified amount to the Policyholder or their heirs. Annuities reverse the principle. Now the buyer pays to the Insurer an amount as capital, in a single or multiple instalments, and the Insurer guarantees to regularly pay back specified amounts after a specified date.

The lines of business are represented diagrammatically below in Figure 21.

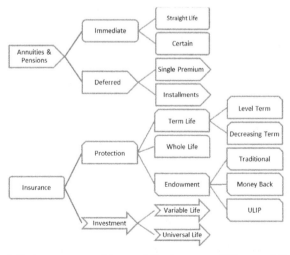

Figure 21: Life Insurance – Lines of Business and Types of Products

Annuities & Pensions

Since Annuities are meant to provide the buyer with the regular payment of a fixed amount once the buyer has attained a specified age they are also called Pension Products. Annuities are of the two main types, but due to a combination of payment options each of the two also has different varieties:

Immediate Payment, or 'Immediate'– the Annuity payments begin immediately after one month, three months, six months one year following the date of purchase,

- *Straight Life, or Immediate:* This type are purchased with a 'single' premium, but the annuities are paid out for the entire lifetime of the purchaser, and cease on his death

- *Certain Period, or 'Certain':* This is similar to the 'Straight Life' type, with a 'Certain' period being chosen during which the annuities are paid to the holder, and if he dies during this period then the payments are made to the designated beneficiary for the remaining period. If the holder survives beyond the certain period the same Annuity continues to be paid to him for life.

Deferred Period or 'Deferred' – the Annuity payments begin after a specified period called the 'Deferred Period,' and can be purchase either with a:

- **Single Premium payment**, or
- **Instalment Payments**, paid periodically

Both of these can be of the 'Certain' type described above. They can also be issued as 'Joint' Plans, when the Annuity continues to be paid to the last surviving holder till his or her death. If the Plans are of the 'with profit' kind or are issued with riders such as 'Accident Benefits,' 'Double Accident Benefits' or "Disability' benefits, then accrual of any Bonus or Rider Benefit payment would add to the quantum of Annuity payment.

Life Insurance Products

The original purpose of life insurance is to offer risk protection in the event of death of the policyholder by providing his survivors with a certain sum of money which would help support them.

We could say that there are basically two families of Life Insurance Products – Protection and Investment Plans, but the families are interrelated, and Protection Plans have variants with elements of investment, and Invest Products also provide a component for risk protection.

Protection Plans

The Term Insurance Policy

'Term' Insurance Policies evolved as basic instruments of risk protection. They cover the risk of life for the term or specified period and pay the benefit if the policy holder dies within this period, at the end of which the 'protection' ceases and no 'benefit' or amount is paid back to the policyholder. They are issued for periods ranging from one to thirty years. Many of the short duration policies carry a 'renewability' clause which means that the policy is renewal for additional terms up to the time of a specified age of the policyholder. The insurer will not deny renewal if the demanded premium is paid by the policyholder. 'Annual Renewable Term' is a common type of term policy where the insurer guarantees reissue of a policy of equal or lesser amount without regard to the question of insurability of the life Assured. The premium payable at each due instalment, from monthly to annual for a policy does not change during the term whatever its duration. But, at each renewal the premium payable would be as applicable for the age of the Assured at time of renewal.

There are two basic kinds of term policies:

- **'Level' Term** – the Sum Assured, or 'Death' benefit stays constant throughout the term, and

- **'Decreasing' Term** – the Death Benefit drops is defined, proportionate decrements every year.

The Whole Life Policy

The Whole Life Policy is another type of 'protection' policy, but without a fixed term. It pays the benefit to the beneficiaries, inheritors or nominee after the death of the policyholder. The premium was originally meant to be paid throughout the life time of the policyholder but modern plans restrict the premium paying term to a specified age. Some altered plans have a maturity age, say 85 years, at which point the policy Sum Assured becomes payable even if the policyholder is alive. At times there is also a provision for payment of Bonus at maturity.

With the passage of time public demand surfaced for a product which besides providing risk protection would also give them some sort of financial return at the end, which would give policyholders a feeling of getting something back for all the premiums paid over the years. Pure Protection plans such as Term and Whole Life Plans left them with the hollow, though irrational, feeling that all the money paid as premium was just a cash outflow with that amorphous feeling of 'security' which in the end was not even needed. They wanted something more, and Insurers came up with Endowment Policies as an answer.

Endowment Policies

Strictly speaking a 'pure' Endowment Plan should provide not risk protection during its term but a capital sum, the 'endowment,' at the end of it. However Endowment Insurance policies are mainly risk protection instruments during their term and which also provide at the end a capital sum pay out which includes the policy sum assured and the accumulated bonus which is declared periodically by the Insurance Company. This is made possible by charging a premium which has two components, one of which, the 'mortality' premium, goes towards covering risk, and the other, the 'savings' component, which builds the maturity value and which is further augmented by profits that accrue to the corpus. In this way the Endowment plan protects the risk of death during its term, and builds a corpus which is paid out at maturity. Compared 'apple to apple,' for the same term and sum assured, the pure 'Term' policies charge the lowest premium, the 'Whole Life' policies also carry low premiums, but Endowment Policies are considerably more expensive. There are 3 different varieties of Endowment with which you should become acquainted:

Traditional Plans – these offered Risk protection for the value of Sum Assured plus accrued Bonus during policy term, and an endowment payment or maturity benefit of Sum Assured plus total Bonus at maturity. The accounting and investment of Savings component was totally the prerogative of the Company and the policyholder was only provided with information of the growth of the policy fund; the lack of transparency and of choice of investment options was the downside offset by an element of certainty of growth of corpus.

Money Back – The 'Money Back' plan became an interesting offering. It combined the component of Risk protection with a series of fixed payouts every few years to the policy holder during the term itself. The customer has the 'feel' of continuous protection and enjoying a cash inflow without having to wait for the policy to mature. While protection continued for the full value of Sum Assured during the policy's term, the policyholder also received at periodic intervals a payout of a portion of the Sum Assured. At maturity he received the balance amount left from the Sum Assured. This looked like 'Insurance Protection for 'nothing' and money for free,' but actually it came at a heavier price than even Traditional Endowment policies. Again, like traditional plans these too also suffered from the same opaqueness, and during bull runs on the stock markets adventurous policyholders felt that greater flexibility and freedom to participate in the markets would have allowed them to reap greater profits. ULIPs were the natural outcome for this search for empowerment and profits with protection.

ULIPs – The Unit Linked Insurance Plan is an endowment product which consists of two distinct parts. The "Risk' coverage forms one part and it is supported by the 'Mortality Charge' collected as a component of the policy premium. The balance premium, less administrative charges, is used to purchase 'Units' of an Investment Fund which is created and managed by the Insurance Company. This Investment Fund is created by pooling policyholder funds which are then invested in different asset classes such as debt market funds, equities, bonds and other asset classes. The units purchased under each policy are held in an attached 'Investment Account.' The policyholder can check his investment account's balance at any given time.

The valuation of the Investment Funds and the Units is maintained and declared on a daily basis by the Insurance Company. The policyholder receives full access to information about the balance in his account, the investments made by the Investment Fund and valuations. Often the Insurance Company maintains several Investment Funds each investing in different types of asset classes. For example a Company may maintain a Conservative Fund which invests mainly is debt instruments and corporate deposits, an Aggressive Fund which invests mainly in equities, and a Balance Fund which invests in a mix of equities and debt instruments. Policyholders are not only allowed to choose at inception which of these Funds they propose to hold their units in, but they are given liberty to reallocate, or 'switch,' their units from one type of fund to the other depending upon expectation of better returns. This creates the feeling of empowerment, which with the transparency in maintenance of fund investments and valuations gives ULIPs the unique flavour of security of risk coverage with the thrill of participation in economic markets.

Investment Plans

Universal Life and Variable Life insurance policies both have a savings account attached to them, and differ in the way the account is managed.

Universal Life Insurance policies are those under which the cash account receives money paid in as premium. The funds which accumulate in the 'cash account' earn interest at a guaranteed minimum 'money market' rates of interest, but the actual rate is usually more. The mortality charge is paid out of the account, and this reduces the account balance. If sufficient balance has accumulated in the account the policyholder can suitably adjust their premium payments into the account downwards, or upwards, and the policy coverage continues. The death coverage is guaranteed, as long as there is sufficient balance in the account to pay the premium.

Variable Life Insurance policies allow the policyholder to allocate premium balances left after mortality charges between one or more cash savings accounts for investment in equities, debt and bonds. While the death benefit is guaranteed the policyholder has the freedom to maximize his gains from investing in financial products.

The difference between these products and the more traditional policies is mostly that emphasis shifts more towards 'investments' and the build up of cash value, leaving the risk coverage as a fixed underlying element.

In the end all life insurance policies, other than pure term plans, are a mix of risk coverage with investment in different proportions and degrees of flexibility and control for the policyholder over the investment portion.

Note: Readers will be interested to note that the General Insurance Industry refers to the the value insured by a policy as the "Sum Insured," whereas the Life Insurance Industry uses the term "Sum Assured" to refer to the value insured. Same concept...... different terms, and we have tried to follow the tradition as faithfully as possible.

CHAPTER 15

Micro Insurance – Prospects at the Bottom of the Pyramid

What is Micro Insurance? Purpose and Objectives;
Sales, Services & Products at the Bottom of the Pyramid;
Mass Health Insurance Schemes & Group Personal Accident Insurance

The Bottom of the Pyramid – Emergence of a New Consumer Segment

For a long time Business Enterprises, Managers and Management Experts did not consider the poor and disadvantaged segments of society as a business segment. They were not regarded as consumers, for it was assumed that they lacked the purchasing power to buy and use the products that industries conventionally produced. This traditional type-casting was destroyed by the work of C.K. Prahalad, an internationally renowned business strategist and thought leader who demonstrated that the lower economic segment of society had latent consumption needs as much as the middle and upper classes, that they had a desire for quality products and services, but required products that were re-designed, engineered and packaged to their specific situation and needs. He supported his theories with the evidence of the pioneering efforts of some innovative Managers who had perhaps unwittingly created products suited to this segment, and had successfully made a profitable business out of their ventures. Prahald called this customer segment the "Bottom of the Pyramid," and since then the nomenclature and classification has become widely accepted. He awakened Industry and the Management fraternity to the possibility of making profits where till then none seemed to exist. The Bottom-of-the-Pyramid (BOP) deserved not 'charity,' but goods and services that gave them real value for their money.[21]

Micro Insurance Business Segment – a Profile

The Micro Insurance business segment owes its origins to Government policy making much more than it does to a conscious adoption of the ideas of CK Prahalad, though the Insurance Industry would certainly benefit immensely by applying his theories.

Micro Insurance may be described as the business of providing insurance protection to "low-income people against specific perils in exchange for regular premium payments proportionate to the likelihood and cost of the risk involved."[22] However, Micro Insurance is often regarded as the distributing of existing insurance products after stripping them of some less necessary features, scaling down the value or Sum Insured and suitably reducing the price to make it 'affordable.' A Micro Insurance policy is treated simply as a low -premium insurance policy, a 'small ticket' size product. This is not correct. Micro Insurance policies are, and have to be, 'small ticket' for the amount of insurance protection required by this segment, the value of the asset that has to be protected and the price they can afford to pay is quite small compared to persons and risks situated further up the economic ladder. However, it is not scale but a number of other and more **important factors which differentiate the needs of the Low-income segment clients:**

Geographical Location: Many live in remote rural areas and require a different distribution channel; it is true that the urban poor are also a part of this segment, but even to service them the traditional products, channels and strategies are not suitable.

Literacy: Members of this segment are often illiterate and unfamiliar with the concept of insurance.

Severity of Hazard: The BOP segment person has to often face more risks than wealthier people do because they may either be exposed to greater 'severity' and variety of hazards , and also because they cannot afford the same defences. For example, on average a poor person is more prone to illness because they do not eat as well, work under more hazardous conditions and do not have regular medical check –ups.

Financial Literacy: BOP people have little or less experience of dealing with formal financial institutions, the documentation and formal processes involved, of their rights and duties as consumers.

Usage Costs: The existing requirements for documentation and processes, which may be routine for educated middle class consumers, would seem to carry hidden time-opportunity costs for BOP persons who may find them daunting. A middle segment policyholder may have little difficulty in filling up detailed 'Claim Forms,' attaching several documents, and emailing a set of scanned copies and sending the originals by post, but this is beyond the horizon for the BOP claimant. He would probably visit a Branch Office in person to transact, to obtain the Forms, then spend more time to get them filled up, probably with the help of someone conversant with them, and finally return to the insurance Office to deposit them. The cost in terms of money, time and lost work opportunity is very high for such a person.

Self evidently, Micro Insurance products have to be designed to incorporate these factors as well as the difference in monetary scale. Simply reducing the price of existing insurance policies, and 'tweaking' the features is an inadequate solution.

A Profile of the Segment

The Micro Insurance segment has not been defined in any Indian Law or Regulation in terms of the levels of income or geographical location. In fact there is no formal definition of such a customer segment. However there is a definition of the 'Rural Sector' in as much as a rural location is defined in terms of population and a target is stipulated for the number of policies which an Insurer must sell in rural locations. The regulations specify that these clients must come from rural areas. With poverty in India largely located in rural areas, the effect of such a stipulation is to ensure that poor clients are sold policies. The urban poor, of which there is also a good number, are not covered specifically by regulations. The Micro Insurance business segment must therefore be understood in terms of its characteristics, risks faced and requirements for protection. There is, however, a regulatory definition of what constitutes a 'micro' general insurance and life insurance product which we will shortly examine.

Using broad generalizations we can build up a profile of the typical client for micro insurance. The chief characteristics of customers of this market segment are:

Family Size: Usually households consist of five or more members, sharing income and access to financial services.

Source of Income: Agricultural labour is the main source of income. However, there is additional income from off-farm activities, and family members pursue multiple activities to supplement income. The implications of this are that much of the income is irregular and seasonal. Premium collection must take into account the particular variances in the seasonal income of this market.

Risk Profile: Due to their poverty they present a higher than average risk profile for many types of insurance. For example, due to lack of sanitation, lack of access to clean water, hazardous working conditions and poor nutrition imply higher rates of death and disease. This means they present a higher risk profile for both Health and Accident insurance.

Literacy: Low levels of literacy imply that marketing needs to be done without written media: for example, film, radio and word of mouth.

Product Distribution profile: The rural poor often live in areas with inadequate road and telecommunications infrastructure, which increases the costs of selling and servicing policies. In urban areas infrastructure is increasingly not a constraint, and only the awareness gap needs to be bridged.

Risks and Vulnerabilities

The poor by definition own very few assets. In contrast to the urban poor, many of the rural poor own their dwelling and the land that it is constructed on. Income generation for the landless poor is largely a function of daily agricultural labour rates and the number of days such work is available.

The insurable perils would be:

- **Loss of life**: Most household members contribute to household income, except those too old, young or infirm to work.

- **Critical illness:** This has the dual impact of loss of earnings, inability to do household labour as well as necessity to incur treatment expenses.

- **Medical Exigencies and Illness**: These reduce the working days and income, and also create expenses though not at the high level of a critical illness.

- **Old Age Pension:** There are few income options during old age, and not enough savings to take care of expenses. Also, there is some evidence of emerging social trends in which the obligation of the young to take care of the old is weakening.

- **Reduction in Agricultural Productivity:** Crop Failure, lowered agricultural productivity or returns caused by low levels of rainfall or natural catastrophes.

- **Loss of Assets:** Damage or destruction of assets used to generate income, or of house and household possessions.

- **Personal Accident and Disability:** Especially among specific occupational groups such as construction workers, or farm labourers working on dangerous machinery such as 'Threshers' or 'Crushers,' accident at the workplace and disability are risks which can destroy lives by eliminating a person's capacity to earn and support himself and his dependants.

Regulatory Specifications – Micro Insurance Products

IRDAI Regulations define two types of micro insurance products:

General Micro Insurance Product, which refers to any policy offering coverage for:

1. 'Health,' with Sum Insured not exceeding 1,00,000/- for Individuals and Sum Insured not exceeding 2,50,000/- for families, or

2. Belongings such as 'Hut,' 'Livestock,' 'Tools or Instruments,' with Sum Insured not exceeding 1,00,000/- per asset, or

3. Personal Accident on Individual, Family or Group basis, with Sum Insured not exceeding 1,00,000/-, and for a fixed period 1 year.

Life Micro Insurance Product, which is specified as any Life Insurance policy that offers

1. 'Life,' or 'Pension' or 'Health' insurance benefits

2. A Sum Insured not exceeding 2,00,000/-

The guidelines also stipulate that the Life Insurance policy should be either a 'Term' or 'Endowment' product but not a 'Unit Linked Insurance Plan' which was specifically prohibited. Payment of Premium in instalments may be permitted except for policies that are regular premium, pure 'Term' or 'Health' products. Endowment Policies could carry standard features such as 'Lock-in' period and 'Surrender Value.'

Product and Their Features

Mass Health Schemes: Rashtriya Swasthya Bima Yojana (RSBY)

For the poor and disadvantaged, people forced to live below the poverty line, an illness is the single biggest threat to their income and their earning capacity. It often leads them and their families in a crushing "debt trap." Fearing the high cost of medical treatment, and the possible loss of wages due to absence from work, they postpone treatment till it is almost too late. The treatment itself can consume their savings, compel them to sell assets, even force them into debt. A well designed, and efficiently executed mass healthcare program can provide the remedy for all these problems. In the past healthcare schemes run by the Central and State Governments had failed to achieve these objectives.[23]

The Rashtriya Swasthya Bima Yojana (RSBY) is a carefully designed healthcare initiative launched by Ministry of Labour and Employment, Government of India on 1st April 2008 that takes care of a very wide range of eventualities with a solution that combines convenience with efficiency, ensuring both security against fraud and freedom from bureaucratic delay.

Features

Sum Insured: Hospitalization coverage up to Rs. 30,000/- is provided for an extremely wide range of diseases.

Treatment Costs: Treatment Protocols have been fixed as a combination of procedures, medicines, tests and stay at a hospital for in-patient treatment. A package rate is fixed by the Government after negotiation with the hospitals for a large number of interventions.

Pre-existing conditions: These are covered from day one and there is no age limit.

Family Coverage: The coverage extends to five members of the family which includes the head of household, spouse and up to three dependents.

Costs

Registration Fee: The Beneficiary has to pay Rs. 30/- as registration fee

Premium: The premium is paid by the Central and State Government to the insurer who is selected by the State Government. on the basis of a competitive bidding process.

Group Size & Membership

Each policy contract was specified to cover an individual district in a state. A single insurance company assumed the liability for each district, and delivered services through an office to be located in the district.

Beneficiary Enrolments: The Insurance Company uses Mobile Enrolment Stations to conduct on-the-spot Enrolment according to well publicized schedules, on the basis of data of Below Poverty Line (BPL) population provided by the State Government. Biometric information (fingerprints) and photographs are taken for the beneficiary and family members. Smart Cards recording the biometric and pictographic information are issued on the spot for beneficiaries and their family members.

Technology Integration: In a unique initiative the Central has deployed state-of-the art technology and processes for a social sector scheme on a pan-India scale. Every beneficiary family is issued a biometric enabled smart card containing their fingerprints and photographs. All the hospitals empanelled under RSBY are IT enabled and connected to the server at the district level. This ensures a smooth data flow regarding service utilization periodically.

Robust Monitoring and Evaluation – RSBY is evolving a robust monitoring and evaluation system. An elaborate backend data management system is being put in place which can track any transaction across India and provide periodic analytical reports. The basic information gathered by government and reported publicly should allow for mid-course improvements in the scheme. It may also contribute to competition during subsequent tender processes with the insurers by disseminating the data and reports.

Security & Fraud-proofing: The biometric enabled smart card ensures that only the real beneficiary can use the smart card. The key management system of RSBY ensures that the card reaches the correct beneficiary and there remains accountability in terms of issuance of the smart card and its usage.

Portability – A beneficiary enrolled in a particular location can use their smart card in any RSBY empanelled hospital across India, a feature especially beneficial for poor families that migrate across geographies due to employment opportunities, e.g. in the construction industry. Cards can also be split for migrant workers to carry a share of the coverage with them separately.

Cash less and Paperless transactions – A RSBY beneficiary receives cashless treatment in any of the empanelled hospitals. Their Smart Card provides verification via their finger prints. For the treatment received the Hospital is paid directly by the Insurer. The Hospital sends the claim 'On-line' to the Insurer and gets paid electronically, and papers do not have to be sent.

Sustainable Business Model – Incentivizing All Stakeholders

The RSBY initiative has been structured as a business model with incentives for each stakeholder to ensure both its future expansion and long run sustainability. Each incentive creates a complementary responsibility or even a countervailing oversight function to keep a check on misuse.

- **Insurers** – Since the Insurance Company is paid premium for each household enrolled it therefore has the motivation to enrol as many households as possible from the BPL list, thus promoting maximum coverage of targeted beneficiaries.

- **Hospitals** – A hospital has the incentive to provide treatment to large number of beneficiaries as it is paid per beneficiary treated. Since both

Public and Private Hospitals can participate in the RSBY Program there shall be healthy competition between them to provide better services. Insurers, in contrast, will monitor participating hospitals in order to prevent unnecessary procedures or fraud resulting in excessive claims.

- **Intermediaries** – Intermediaries such as NGOs and MFIs which have a greater stake in assisting BPL households as they will be paid for the services they render in reaching out to the beneficiaries.
- **Government** – By paying only a maximum sum up to Rs. 750/- per family per year, an amount that would be reduced through competitive bidding, the Government would be able to provide below poverty line household with access to quality health care.

Unlike many government initiatives in the past, the RSBY program has combined innovation, advanced technology and meticulous design to deliver healthcare to the poor sections of society.

The World Bank, the UN and the ILO praised RSBY as one of the world's best health insurance schemes, and Germany is evaluating how it may adopt or adapt the smart card based model for revamping its own social security system.[24]

This is a level of efficiency that is still not rivalled by the conventional health products sold by Insurance Companies to customers from higher economic segments. It would seem less likely, but this once at least, the advanced management concepts of CK Prahald have received concrete shape not from the work of a Corporate Giant but through the efforts of a Government Department.

Group Personal Accident Insurance Schemes

An example of a Group Personal Accident Insurance product designed for the 'Micro' insurance segment is the **Pradhan Mantri Suraksha Bima Yojna (PMSBY) Policy** which has been discussed in Chapter 13. It offers Personal Accident insurance of a fixed and limited Sum Insured to Bank Account holders residing in both urban and rural locations who voluntarily choose to join the scheme. The premium has been pegged at an affordable minimum while the documentation and procedure is relatively simple. The Banks are authorized to choose the Insurer who will administer the scheme, issue policies and deliver services, with the Banks acting as a 'Single-point-of-Contact' for enrolling their account holders and for service delivery.

Insurance of Agriculture – Crop Insurance & Weather Insurance

Effect of Weather and Rainfall on Agricultural output

All over the world farmers have to face the risk of their crops, and yields, being adversely affected by variable weather conditions. In India agriculture is even more dependent on weather in general, and rainfall in particular, and this further increases the risks for the farm sector. In addition, the limited means of a majority of farmers reduces their ability to cope with the consequences of adverse weather on farm outputs. Together these two factors can have disastrous consequences for agriculture.

History of Crop Insurance in India

Crop Insurance started in 1972–73 with some pilot projects which led to the Comprehensive Crop Insurance Scheme which lasted from 1985 to 1999 when it was succeeded by the National Agricultural Insurance Scheme (NAIS). In 2003 'Weather' Insurance, a totally new product widely regarded as a superior solution to the existing yield-based products was launched by ICICI Lombard in Mahboobnagar district of Andhra Pradesh. Quickly, in 2004–05, similar products were quickly launched by IFFCO-Tokio General Insurance (ITGI) and The Agricultural Insurance Company of India (AIC), the Public Sector Insurer.

Types of Crop Insurance

Broadly speaking there are two types of Crop Insurance Products:

- **Yield based:** Compensation is offered for the actual reduction in crop output compared to a pre-settled benchmark. The National Agricultural Insurance Scheme (NAIS) is an example of this type.

- **Weather Index based:** Compensation is made for the fluctuation in weather beyond fixed parameters, without the tedious and difficult process of measuring actual fall in yield. This is done on the basis of a pre-established correlation between various weather parameters and crop output for notified homogenous areas which are exposed to similar weather conditions, have similar soil fertility and output.

At present Crop Insurance, whether under the NAIS or Weather Index products is compulsory for farmers who have taken crop loans from Banks. They have to join whichever scheme is extended for their location. Other farmers, who have not taken a loan, have the option to join one or the other if both are available.

It should be noted that Crop Insurance is a 'work-in-progress,' a product under continuous evolution and improvement. The Government and the Regulator constantly attempt to learn from experience and successively provide better features to farmers. The NAIS has been replaced by the Pradhan Mantri Fasal Bima Yojna (PMFSBY) with upgraded features.

117

However, to build an understanding of the subject and the two different types we will base our analysis on the NAIS Scheme on the one hand and the WBCIS on the other.

The National Agriculture Insurance Scheme (NAIS) – an Evaluation

The NAIS is operated on the basis of the 'area approach' under which homogenous areas are defined as insurance units. These could be either a District, a Tlauka, a Block, a Mandal, a Circle, a Gram Panchayat, or village etc. When the season's average yield per hectare of the insured crop for the defined unit falls below the guaranteed yield all the insured farmers in the defined area get the same indemnity per unit of Sum Insured.

All the states except Punjab, Arunachal Pradesh, Manipur and Nagaland have implemented the scheme. Studies reveal that a large number of the farmers who benefitted from the scheme belonged to the 'small and marginal' category. However, despite encouraging results from the point of view of 'socio-economic equity' an analysis of the penetration levels across regions and crops does not show very impressive results.

Even after more than two decades of the NAIS, less than one-fifth of the farmers in the country are insured. Rajasthan, where about 50% of the farmers/holdings are insured, is one of the few notable exceptions. Apparently, the scheme has not proved a significant risk mitigation tool for farmers in many regions. Possible reasons for this are

1. The high 'actuarial' rates of premium charged
2. Lack of coverage for perennial crops, fruits and vegetables
3. Failure of many implementing states to move down to the lower insurance units like villages to minimize 'basic' risk
4. The Low, and unappealing, 'guaranteed yields' on the basis of which claims are paid out
5. The failure to make timely indemnity payouts at the time of crop failures.

The biggest disadvantage of the yield based scheme is the delayed claim settlement procedure. This often takes at least a year, denying the insured the benefit of insurance when it matters the most, and in the end negating the very object of insurance. The delay is the result of the time taken for the crop cutting experiments (CCE) data to be collated and the inability of the state and central governments to contribute their share towards claim settlements.

Weather Based Crop Insurance Scheme (WBCIS) – an Emerging Alternative

Weather Based Crop Insurance Scheme (WBCIS) does not pay claims on the basis of actual losses experienced by the Insured as is done by the yield based insurance schemes. Compensation is made for the realisation or failure of a weather index that is highly correlated with actual losses. The index measures a specific weather variable (e.g. rainfall, temperature, relative humidity, wind speed, etc.). The WBCIS also utilizes the concept of 'area approach. The insurance covers distinct units termed as a Reference Unit Area (RUA) each of which is linked to a Reference Weather Station (RWS). All the farmers in a given RUA are deemed to have suffered the same level of adverse weather incidence and are equally eligible for the indemnity. WBCIS is based on actuarial rates of premium.

The design of the weather product is based on analysis of the data of weather parameters that affect crop growth in its three critical phases – 1) sowing, 2) growth and flowering, and 3) yield formation to harvest. For each of these periods a 'Trigger' and 'Exit' level is determined for the chosen weather parameter and notified in the policy. When the Trigger is breached and the Index crosses it upwards or downwards as the case may be, a specified claim payment is made to the farmer. When the Index crosses the Exit levels the farmer gets the maximum payouts. Further deterioration of the Index does not lead to any more payout for the maximum indemnity has already been paid.

Advantages

Weather insurance has some specific advantages over traditional yield based insurance:

- **Coverage of New Crops:** insurance can now also be provided for crops with no historical yield data as also for horticultural crops, whereas yield based insurance requires historical data of yields to determine what the standard yield is, and to calculate premium rates.

- **Timely Claims Payment:** Claim payouts are automatically triggered once the weather parameter reaches the pre-specified level. Under the yield based scheme claim settlement is delayed as the procedure takes about a year due to Crop Cutting Experiments (CCE), Collation of Data, delay by state and central governments to contribute their share towards claim settlements.

- **Lower Cost and Less Complicated Program Administration**: WBCIS is more cost effective and simple to administer. Costly field visits are not required. The problem of 'Moral Hazard' and 'Adverse Selection' is reduced as the Insured is not likely to have better information than the insurer about the underlying index nor would he be in a position to influence the realisation of the index. Most of all, the product can be reinsured in the International Markets unlike the NAIS which has unsustainably high claim ratios.

Disadvantages

There are some major constraints associated with these products:

- **Spatial variations in weather parameters** are high in India and basis risk can only be minimized if claims structures are worked out at smaller units than at present. Presently weather data is often recorded at taluka level. The actual impact of adverse weather condition at the farm location may be significantly different from that recorded by the RWS.

- **Poor density of weather stations** has led to high basis risks, and paucity of weather data in certain regions has made it difficult to extend the scheme to many new areas.

- **High Start-up Cost:** Installing a large number of new weather stations, which is necessary to bring down the basis risk to an acceptable level, would also result in high start-up costs.

Cattle & Livestock Insurance has been briefly discussed in Chapter 13 and the features mentioned there need not be repeated here.

Distribution Channels

The Partnership Model; The Micro Agency Model; Effect of the Quota System

There are two models, or channels, for distribution of Micro Insurance products, the Partnership Model and the Micro Agency Model. Both have their advantages and difficulties.

The Partnership Model is based on a partnership between the insurer and an organization that provides some kind of financial service to large numbers of low-income people, for example a Microfinance organization, an NGO, or a business that supplies agricultural goods such as a fertilizer supplier. The Organization acts as an Agent and sells insurance policies to the clients on behalf of the Insurer.

The Insurer utilizes the established distribution channels of this agent to reach low-income groups, without having to incur the high costs of setting up their own distribution network. The Agent is able to maximize their revenue earnings through the opportunity to cross-sell insurance products.

The partnership model utilizes the comparative strengths of both partners, leaving each free to focus on their core business. While the Insurer takes up the risk management function, bears the risk, handles product development, claims processing and payment, and the investment of reserves, the Agent acts as the distribution arm and service provider. The Agent distributes the product, uses their infrastructure for product servicing, brand building, marketing the product, premium collection, and assists in claims management.

An example of the Partnership Model in India is BASIX, an NGO working in livelihood promotion in several arid and backward districts spread over seven states. BASIX works towards its mission of livelihood promotion by providing a comprehensive set of services, which include Livelihood Financial Services (Savings, Credit and Insurance) and Institutional Development Services. BASIX is headquartered at Hyderabad. As part of its mission to deliver comprehensive financial services to rural customers, BASIX began its initiatives to deliver insurance services four years ag o, coinciding with the opening up of the insurance sector. From the beginning, BASIX has actively partnered with multiple insurance companies to design insurance products for rural customers. In the area of life insurance BASIX began by working with ICICI Prudential and currently works with AVIVA Life Insurance Company. BASIX has worked with Royal Sundaram General Insurance Company for the delivery of livestock insurance and ICICI Lombard for rainfall insurance. In 2003, BASIX was also given a Corporate Agency license by the IRDAI to distribute retail life insurance products from AVIVA.

There is, however, a shortcoming of this model which should also be mentioned. The Insurer is dependent on the quality of the agent, and NGOs in particular are often 'here today, gone tomorrow,' relying on donor recognition and goodwill for their survival.

Micro-Agent Model

The micro-agent model: How does it work?

While the partnership model is relatively common, the micro -agent model described below is unique. It is the invention of Tata -AIG, specifically an employee of Tata-AIG, Vijay Artherye.

The central building blocks of the model are Rural Community Insurance Groups (CRIGs) supervised by rural organizations such as churches, NGOs or MFIs. CRIGs are a partnership firm formed of five women from a self -help group (SHG). The leader of the CRIG is licensed as an agent. The CRIG is a de facto brokerage firm (in the functional, not the legal sense of the term).

All CRIGs in the same geographic area meet in a single centre, usually organized with the assistance of the rural organization, and receive training and assistance from Tata -AIG. This practice reduces training costs.

Micro-Agent Model: Profile and Workings of a Typical CRIG

Most CRIGs consist of four to five members. These members are usually women who are part of an SHG. The typical profile of a member would include communication skills, acceptance of insurance, preferably educated up to the 10th standard, with influence in the SHGs, and capable of doing some paperwork. The CRIG has a leader appointed by Tata -AIG on the advice of the rural organization. A typical leader will be educated to the 12th standard or above, have a good track record of past social -sector performance and integrity, be systematic and organized, with leadership qualities, and public speaking and training skills. This leader is trained by Tata -AIG to obtain a corporate agent's license. The CRIG as a whole is registered as a body under the Andhra Pradesh Societies Act (where the model is currently being used).

The CRIG leader and members are involved in promotion, sales and collection of insurance proceeds and maintaining records. The CRIG leader will document all fortnightly CRIG meetings and all weekly meetings with the NGO concerned.

While it is true that insurance of rural assets and crops started over four decades ago, the identification of 'Bottom of the Pyramid' segment and focused development of micro insurance products for its specific needs is a recent phenomenon. Micro Insurance presents the Insurance industry with unique challenges and opportunities. If the Insurance Industry is successful, like the FMCG Industry, in innovatively developing products and service delivery mechanisms for this segment, it shall have carried insurance to a 'next' level of growth and provided risk management solutions to those who need it most but have the least access to it.

References

1. Kashyap, Anthony and Krech; Microinsurance: Demand and Market Prospects – India; 2006; Federal Ministry for Economic Cooperation and Development, Germany; http://www.undp.org/content/dam/aplaws/publication/en/publicat ions/capacity-development/microinsurance-demand-and-market-prospects-for-india/Microinsurance.pdf]

2. Reshmy Nair; Crop Insurance in India: Changes and Challenges; Economic and Political Weekly; 6th February, 2010; VOL XLV No.6

3. Rajeev Ahuja, Basudeb Guha-Khasnobis; Micro-Insurance In India: Trends And Strategies For Further Extension; June 2005; Indian Council For Research On International Economic Relation; Working Paper No.162

CHAPTER 16
Policy Servicing – in Life and General Insurance

The Insurance Policy Document, Policy Servicing in General Insurance and Life Insurance Business; Regulatory Guidelines

Insurance is widely, and correctly, regarded as a long term business, one which commences with the sale of a product but is expected to develop into a strong relationship of mutual trust between the buyer and seller, that stretches long beyond the time horizon of normal financial products. Very often, the business operates true to this paradigm and is able to create durable relationships with customers. In this chapter we shall discuss the activity of policy servicing, and how it has an impact on the creation of stable relationships with customers.

Many employees and distribution agents regard the insurance policy as an important component of the service they deliver to customers. In reality the insurance policy is the equivalent of the 'warranty card,' the operational manual and the 'invoice' which a customer gets every time he purchases something, be it a gadget, clothes, or some consumable. Providing these to a customer is necessary to establish the terms of sale, the conditions that apply, the duties and rights of each party to the transaction. Of course, the policy has a higher legal status since it is a formal contract, but it would be best to regard it functionally in the same way as these documents.

The Insurance Policy Document

The insurance policy is the record of the 'product specifications,' of what has been bought and sold, the extent and limitations, and the manner in which the services can be accessed and delivered. It is valid for the 'duration' or 'period of insurance,' the time frame for which the insurer has assumed the risk.

Contract Wordings: Both the Life Insurance and General Insurance policy consists of two parts. The first consists of pre-printed, standard 'Clauses' and 'Conditions' which are common for all policies issued for a particular product, and are commonly referred to as the 'Contract,' 'Bond,' 'Wordings' or even just as the 'Policy.'

Add On Covers and Riders: In addition to the standard coverage offered in what we may call the 'base' version of the policy by borrowing a phrase from the auto industry, Insurers offer enhancements called 'Add-Ons' by the General Insurance Industry and 'Riders' by the Life Insurance Industry. These require special definition of what is being provided, and they too could either be included in main body of the first part of the Policy Document, or on separate sheets. The 'wordings' of the 'Add On' or Rider are called 'Endorsements,' a term which is also used for documents issued to make mid-term changes to a policy.

The Schedule: The so-called second part of the policy, is called the 'Schedule,' and this records the individual details of each policy holder, which vary with each policy sold to a customer.

Policy Servicing – General Insurance

General Insurance policies are issued for a period of one year or less. There are some notable exceptions to this norm, such as policies insuring projects under construction, policies for some types of cargo in transit, and a few 'health insurance' or 'dwelling insurance' policies which are sometimes issued for slightly longer durations. However, the great majority of these policies are valid for a period of one year or less. During this period, on occasion, the circumstances of the 'risk' can change. Mentioned below are some of the more **common types of changes** that are required by policyholders:

- **Sale, Purchase or Change in Ownership**: for example sale of a Motor vehicle or Building; purchase of a new vehicle to replace an old vehicle; the fitment of a new gadget or accessory to vehicle

- **Addition, Improvements, or Deletion**: Additions to a building or plant and machinery under property insurance policies; Addition of a new member or employee to a 'group policy, or deletion of an employee who has resigned

- **Change in Value**: due to addition to the stock, building or other property

- **Change of Address for Communication**, or other contact details under all types of policies

- **Correction of Description**: correction of description of risk due to accidental data entry errors

- **Cancellation of Policy**: due to change of ownership or cessation of risk

In short, mid-term changes may be required for any number of reasons, and sometimes additional premium, or a processing fee, may have to be collected for this purpose.

The policyholder is expected to make a complete declaration of the facts and requirements for change to the Insurer who collects necessary premium. To make the changes a new policy is not issued to replace the old document, but an Endorsement is issued. This is a document which records the changes being made and is treated as an addition to the policy.

Well before the end of the policy period Insurance Companies send a **'Renewal Notice'** to the policy holders. This is usually a letter, a reminder and invitation to the policy holder to renew the insurance. It mentions details such as the Sum Insured, Premium and the date on which the existing policy will end. While it is not a legal requirement, for obvious reasons related to retention of business and customers the Insurance Companies place great emphasis on ensuring that their Customers get Renewal Notices sufficiently in advance, and make strenuous efforts to collect the Renewal premium before a policy 'expires.' This 'seamless' renewal of insurance benefits both parties. It provides continuous protection for the policy holder and helps the insurer retain business and customer base. A gap between 'expiry' and 'renewal' could create a dangerous window during which there is no insurance protection for the asset. A high level of business retention provides a stable foundation to which addition of new customers adds incremental value in much the same way as 'compound interest' adds to the corpus invested with a Bank. It is also well established that the cost of 'acquiring' new customers is considerably higher than that of retaining existing ones.

'Renewal' is a phenomenon and term associated with the General Insurance industry, and it presents the customer with an opportunity to review the quality and price of his insurance protection. Customers tend to bargain hard at the time of renewal, and Insurers do their utmost to retain them. The constant affirmation of trust and service provides the basis for a long-term relationship.

Policy Servicing – Life Insurance

The Paradigm for the Life Insurance Industry is totally different. Since life insurance policies are invariably issued for long-term periods they do not require 'renewal' (barring one solitary exotic exception). However, the industry does experience a periodic 'activity' and 'moment' when the relationship between insurer and policyholder requires reaffirmation. This happens because, though the policy contract is issued for a long duration and is not subject to renewal, but the premium has to be paid at periodic intervals, varying from 'monthly,' 'quarterly' , 'six-monthly' or 'annually.' The only exception is that curiosity, the 'single premium policy, where the premium, usually a huge sum, is paid at the beginning itself, with nothing to be collected subsequently. These form a very small portion of the sales turnover for reasons discussed elsewhere.

The periodic collection of premium presents a challenge for the Insurance company, though this is much lesser than that posed by the 'renewal' to its' General Insurance counterpart. While the 'Life' policy holder cannot change his company, since the contract is for a long term, the Insurer must ensure that he pays premium before time, or definitely within the 'grace period.' In any case, if the premium is not paid when due, the policy lapses and the protection becomes inoperative. It can be 'revived,' but the procedure is cumbersome and most policies that lapse are not revived. This is a loss to both parties. For the policyholder a 'lapsed' policy is a loss of coverage and of the entire premium paid till that point. For the Insurer it is a loss of a customer and a regular cash stream.[25]

The Insured may fail to pay the premium for a variety of reasons:

- **Fortuitous:** ranging from carelessness, inadvertence, or even plain forgetfulness
- **Financial Incapacity:** Shortage of funds due to other financial needs
- **Value Mismatch:** Excessive High Premium arising from over-purchase of insurance beyond economic capacity; sometimes this is also called 'over selling'
- **Product Mismatch:** dissatisfaction with the product, which is usually caused by 'Miss selling,' which happens when a seller is keen to sell a product which the buyer may not actually need; unscrupulous sellers may overemphasize some features, not reveal restrictive features, may portray the product as more attractive than it is, or may simply 'push' the prospect with persistence and a play on 'emotions'

Insurance companies try to reduce the impact of these factors through pro-active steps. They send Renewal Notices and regular Reminders through electronic media to ensure that fortuitous factors do not prevent renewal. Life Insurance policies provide the facility to pay premium in monthly, quarterly and instalments of other durations. Some types of Life Insurance policies (other than pure 'Term' policies) also provide the Insured with the facility to take a loan proportionate to the paid up value. To prevent value mismatch Agents, Advisors and other Intermediaries are trained to provide skilled assistance to an Insured in choosing the most suitable product and amount according to their needs and larger financial goals. Some companies also run publicity campaigns to create awareness about products, features and factors that should guide buyers in making product selection. Intermediaries are counselled and trained in customer centric behaviour to ensure that they understand the importance of providing correct and meaningful inputs to customers. Internal penalties and deterrents are also put in place to discourage distribution personnel from pushing customers into buying products they do not need but which the distributors want to sell. All of this is done with the objective of preventing miss-selling, which in the long run erodes customer confidence like little else can. Ultimately, however, miss-selling is the outcome of ethical failure on the part of both the individuals who make up the sales force and their organisations, and only a unified resolve and concerted action on the part of both can prevent it.

Regulatory Guidelines

Deeply conscious of the need to ensure that policyholders receive services that meet at least some minimum standards both in terms of policy servicing and payment of claims the IRDAI issued the "Protection of Policy Holders Interests Regulations" in 2002, and subsequently revised and reissued them in 2017. These regulations define the quality and timelines to be followed by all Life and Non-Life Insurers. Some of the significant guidelines for Policy Servicing are summarized below[26]:

- **The Prospectus:** For every product the Prospectus shall explain in simple terms the benefits, coverage, exceptions and conditions.

- **The Proposal Form:** A Proposal Form, to be filled up by the Insured, must be used to record the details of the risk or property that is proposed for insurance, except in the case of Marine insurance for which such forms are traditionally not used. Wherever a Proposal form is not used, e.g. in cases of tele-underwriting, the insurer shall record the information obtained orally in writing, and confirm it within a period of 15 days.

- **The Policy:** Detailed stipulation are made about details which must be mentioned such as the coverage, exclusions, conditions, period of insurance, Sum Insured, premium, etc.

- **Free Look Period (Life Policy):** The insurer must inform the insured in writing at the time of forwarding the policy that the Insured has a period of 15 days after receipt of the policy document during which he may review the terms and conditions, and if not satisfied with them, he has the option to return the policy to the Insurer. In the case of Electronic policies or those obtained through 'distance' mode, this 'Free look' period is extended to 30 days. The Insured will be entitled to a full refund of premium subject only to specified deductions.

- **General Insurance Policy:** In addition to the other requirement applicable to all policies mentioned above, General Insurance policies must also state action to be taken by the insured upon occurrence of a claim, the Insured's post-loss obligation regarding the subject matter of insurance, the provision for cancellation of the policy on grounds of mis-representation, fraud, non-disclosure of material facts or non-cooperation of the insured, etc.

What is more important than the details of the requirements is the fact that the Regulator has taken pro-active steps to protect the rights of policyholders to receive a minimum standard of service, and made defaulting insurance companies subject to strict action and penalties.

CHAPTER 17
Claim Settlement – in Life and General Insurance

It is said that no two claims are the same, for such is the variety of circumstances surrounding events which appear to be similar. Yet, to deliver value to claimants in a consistent and continuous manner, Insurance Companies adopt Standard Operating Procedures (SOPs), using assembly line methodology to handle the uniqueness, complexity and variability of accidental events. However, the achievement of equity and customer satisfaction depends even more on the application of the famed 'Basic Principles' of Insurance, and 'common sense' than on technology or processes.

Life Insurance Claim Settlement

A Life Insurance Policy, as also a General Insurance Policy, is judged by the market in terms of that unwritten rule that a 'financial instrument has value only if it pays the customer at the appointed time.'[27] There are basically two types of Life Insurance Products, firstly the Term and Whole Life policies, and secondly the Endowment and Unit Linked Plans. Under the first type claims are payable only at Death of the policyholder, and under the second in addition to Death claims, payments may arise at other events.

Types of Claims

The types of Claims can therefore be classified as follows:

- **Death Claims** – under Term Policies, Whole Life Insurance Policies, Endowment Plans and ULIPs
- **Maturity Benefit Claims** – Endowment Plans and ULIPs
- **Survival Benefit Claims** – Special Endowment Plans as 'Money Back' at periodic intervals
- **Surrender Claims** – payment of surrender value on demand at eligibility
- **Rider Benefits** – for Critical Illness or Accident riders on demand at contingency

- **Annuity Payments** – periodic after attachment (date on which Annuity payments start)

Documentation and Procedure

While Death claims have to be submitted by the Nominees or Assigns under the policy, the others can only be submitted by the policyholder. The procedure and documentation is relatively simple with a Claim Form, Death Certificate (for death claims) and the Discharge Voucher being the main documents required. Importantly, for Death, Surrender and Maturity claims the original Policy also has to be surrendered. Rider Benefit claims require submission of additional proof of occurrence.

The efficiency of an Insurance Company is really measured by how effectively it handles the settlement of claims. As Maturity and Survival Benefit claims become payable on specified dates already recorded in the policy Companies take pro-active steps like contacting the policyholder well in advance through alerts delivered by Post, email, SMS and even telephone to ensure that the procedure gets completed in time and the maturity proceeds are available with the claimants as soon as possible after the maturity dates. Sometimes, however, claims have to be investigated for possible fraudulent acts, such as fabrication of death certificates, falsification of date of death, attempt at converting a natural death into an accidental death to avail additional value under a rider benefit, etc. The companies try to handle these expeditiously but such cases take time. It is revealing that in 2012–13 the LIC paid 97.63 per cent of the Death Claims submitted and repudiated only 1.12 per cent. The Private Sector Insurers, on the other hand paid 88.65 per cent claims and repudiated 7.85 per cent. Together the two categories are a little less than the natural value of 100%, the difference being the claims under consideration at the end of the year.

The decision making process follows the path of checking the validity of the policy, its coverage of the event on which the claim is based, the entitlement of the person submitting the claim, and an evaluation of the validity and reliability of the documents submitted.

To ensure standardization and speed of service delivery IRDAI has issued specific regulations which are discussed a little later in this chapter.

General Insurance Claim Settlement

The Claims Process

The process followed for Settlement of Claims has already been described in Chapter 5. To recap, it consisted of Claim Intimation, Claim Registration, Survey of Loss, Assessment of Claim, and Disbursement. It is quite possible to further subdivide it into more steps or use different names, but in essence these adequately describe the activity from end-to-end. We will not, therefore, again discuss the Claims Process here, but instead shall add to it with some information about the different Types of Losses, the Decision Making Process, and Regulatory Guidelines to complete the picture.

Types of Losses

The various Lines-of-Business use nomenclature suitable to their type of business to describe different losses or claims:

Motor Insurance, Property Insurance

Total Loss – a total destruction of the insured property which stops existing or as the original object, and is beyond repair, or is so badly damaged that repair would amount to a 'rebuild'

Constructive Total Loss – the property is so badly damaged that the cost of repairs would be 'uneconomical,' either the cost would exceed the insured value, or in the case of Motor Insurance a CTL is declared when repair costs would exceed 75% of the insured value; a CTL is also accepted when the property becomes lodged in a position from which it cannot be retrieved though it may not be otherwise extensively damaged, e.g. a car which falls into a deep mountain gorge from where it cannot be extracted though it is visible and largely intact

Partial Loss – Loss of parts or even total loss of particular portions, or destruction of some functionality; the property is in a condition when it can be repaired at acceptable cost and restored to its original condition and functionality

Marine Cargo Insurance

Total Loss & Constructive Total Loss – as already described above

Particular Average – a term peculiar to cargo insurance, it is used for partial losses as described above

General Average – a type[1] of loss that is only associated with Marine insurance, it occurs when during a voyage a common danger threatens the safety of the voyage itself, and voluntarily or willingly some cargo has to sacrificed, destroyed or thrown away to save the rest; for example, in such a situation some cargo may have to be thrown overboard to lighten the ship and restore buoyancy during a storm that threatens to sink the ship and all aboard it

Health Insurance

Hospitalisation – a medical episode during which the Insured is admitted to a Hospital for a minimum period of twenty-four hours to receive medical treatment which can only be administered at a hospital.

Day Care Treatment – a medical episode which originally required treatment after hospitalisation, but the procedure for which has now become shortened to less than twenty-four hours due to advancement in technology and procedures, e.g. cataract, lithotripsy, laparoscopic surgery. The patient receives treatment at the Hospital but is discharged from it in less than 24 hours from admittance.

Domestic Hospitalisation – a situation arising when either the medical condition of the patient is so serious that shifting him to a hospital may threaten his well-being, and the treatment has to be delivered at home itself by creating a 'hospital' like environment, or it may occur when no bed is vacant in hospital wards to accommodate the patient

Pre-Hospitalisation & Post-Hospitalisation – the treatment, consultation and diagnostic tests which are necessary both before Doctors determine that treatment requires hospitalization, and which have to be conducted to monitor recovery after discharge from hospitalisation

Personal Accident Insurance

Death – compensation claims for death caused by an accidental occurrence

Disability

- **Permanent Total** – a condition when the Insured is totally disabled, e.g. has lost the use of any two limbs (hands or legs) or the sight of both eyes, or a limb and an eye

- **Permanent Partial** – a condition when any one limb or eye has become totally dysfunctional, or of stages of loss of functionality of some limb or eye

- **Temporary Total** – a condition when the Insured is totally disabled for a temporary period, from which he will restored to normal health after medical treatment

Liability Insurance

Torts – losses arising out of civil 'wrongs' or failures of contractual liability, e.g. liability of house's owner to a member of the public injured by object which falls out from the premises, or the liability of a Doctor or Hospital to deliver appropriate medical care resulting in some damage to the health of a patient

Statutory Liabilities – losses arising out of failure to discharge a statutory responsibility, e.g. the liability of a factory owner to provide compensation to a workman injured in an accident while unloading cargo at the factory site.

The Decision Making Process

The most important part of the entire activity of Claim Settlement is the decision whether the claim is payable or not. This is the start of the so-called 'moment of truth' which many people consider to be the defining experience for the consumer and the insurer. The decision itself is the outcome of a fairly structured process which is designed in such a way that it will consistently deliver correct results if it is followed meticulously. The two most vital documents used are a copy of the Insurance Policy and the Survey Report .The Claim Form is also important as it records the Insured's official narration of the loss and how it occurred. Additionally any other documents, Bills of Expenses, etc. submitted by the Claimant in support of his claim are also used to decide:

Checking the Underwriting

Step 1: Is the policy valid and effective – does it cover the date on which the loss has occurred?

Step 2: What is the Cause of Loss – as narrated in the Claim Form and the Survey Report, is the cause of Loss a peril covered by the policy; is coverage established or is further investigation required

Step 3: Is the Subject Matter Covered by the Policy – ensure that the particular item or person for which or who the claim is made is specifically included in the policy?

Step 4: Is any Exclusion Condition operative during loss? Is any circumstance, occurrence or factor operating at the time of loss, an 'Exclusion' under the policy? This will may the claim 'not payable.'

Checking the Loss Assessment

Step 5: Is the Proof of Loss adequate – is the occurrence of loss established, or disproved?

Generally, the 'onus of proof' that a loss has occurred lies on the claimant who must give adequate evidence that a loss has occurred; this is usually done through production of physical evidence of damaged items, inspection and Survey, pictures,

Police Reports, Medical Reports, Books of Accounts, etc as applicable. The 'onus of proof' lies on the Insurance Company to show that the loss has not occurred if it disputes the statements and evidence of the claimant.[28]

Step 6: What is the Quantum of Loss as assessed by the Surveyor?

Step 7: Is the Sum Insured by the Policy adequate to cover the Quantum of Loss assessed?

Evaluating the Claim

If the Policy is valid and effective, covers the subject matter, and covers the peril which caused the loss, if no policy condition has been broken and if no excluded peril, factor or act has operated to cause the loss , then the Claim becomes payable. If the answer to any of these questions is no, the Claim is not payable.

The amount payable depends on the actual value of the damage or loss and whether the Sum Insured under the policy was adequate to cover this amount, otherwise the loss amount is proportionately reduced

Admission or Repudiation of Liability

Step 8: Recording and Approving the Decision – the result of the evaluation has to be recorded in the media or system application preferred by the Company to process its claims transaction; the evaluation is then approved, or rejected, by the Manager who has been given adequate decision taking powers for the amount and type of claim.

Step 9: Communication with Claimant – the communication of acceptance, or rejection, of the claim and the amount payable, to the claimant is the final action which completes the decision making process.

Now the implementation of the decision is done through other standard operating procedures designed for this purpose.

Regulatory Guidelines

The "Protection of Policy Holders Interests Regulations," initially issued by IRDAI in 2002 and then re-issued in 2017, also contain guidelines that define the quality and timelines for the settlement of both Life Insurance and General Insurance claims. Some of the more significant guidelines are summarized below:[29]

Life Insurance Claims

- **Documents in support of Claim:** The Insurance Policy shall state the primary documents which are normally required to be submitted by a claimant in support of a claim.

- **Additional Documents:** Queries or requirements of additional Documents shall be raised all at once and not in piece-meal, within 15 days of receipt of a claim.

- **Death Claims:** Pay, or dispute a claim, giving relevant reasons within 30 days from receipt of all relevant papers and clarifications.

  △ **Investigation:** If an investigation is required it should be initiated at the earliest and completed no later than 90 days from the time the claim is lodged, and the claim shall be settled within 30 days of the completion of investigation.

- **Maturity Claims, Survival Benefit Claims and Payment of Annuities:** Initiate Claim Settlement Process sufficiently in advance to enable payment through Post-Dated Cheques (PDC) or Electronic Transfer directly to Bank Accounts of Beneficiary by 'Due Date.'

- **Amount Held in Trust – Payment of Interest:** If there is any question about proper identification of the payee, the amount should be held for the benefit of the payee at a rate of interest that is applicable to the savings bank accounts.

- **Delay by Insurer:** If there is a delay on the part of the Insurer, they shall pay to the claimant a rate of interest of 2% more than that applicable to a Savings Bank Account. This Interest amount shall be paid by the Insurer 'suo moto,' irrespective of whether it is demanded by the Beneficiary or not.

General Insurance Claims

- **Appointment of Surveyor:** A Surveyor must be appointed within 72 hours of the intimation of a claim. The Insurer must immediately convey to the Claimant details of the appointment, the role, duties and responsibilities of Surveyor, by email or letter.

- **Requirement of Documents:** Within 7 days of Claim Intimation, the Insurer or Surveyor will inform the Claimant of the essential documents to be submitted in support of his claim. If the documents are available in the Public Domain or with Public Authority, then the Surveyor shall collect them.

- **Conduct of Survey**

  △ **Commencement of Survey:** Immediately on appointment, but in no case later than 48 hours the Surveyor shall commence the Survey.

  △ **Interim Report:** A Report of the physical details of the loss shall be submitted by the Surveyor to the Insurer within 15 days of commencement of Survey. The Insurer must provide the Claimant, on his request, a copy of the Interim Report.

  △ **Non-cooperation, by Claimant:** Incomplete Information: Written Intimation to be given to Claimant by Insurer & Surveyor, giving reasons and information about delay in Loss Assessment

- **Final Report of Loss Assessment by Surveyor:** The Surveyor must submit his Assessment Report to the Insurer within a stipulated time:

  △ Within 30 days of his appointment for all normal claims.

  △ Within 90 days for all Commercial and Large Risks, the Surveyor must submit the Final Report to the Insurer with a Copy to Insured, on request.

  △ Within Extended period specially permitted by an Insurer for complicated claims or those involving complex questions about Reinstatement/ Replacement. Fortnightly 'Status Reports' will have to submitted by the Surveyor.

- **Additional Survey Report:** If more information is required, the Insurer may seek a maximum of only one Additional Report per claim, within 15 days of submission of a Final Report. The Surveyor must submit this Additional Report within 3 weeks of request by Insurer.

- **Settlement of Claim by Insurer:** The Insurer must 'Accept' or 'Repudiate' a Claim within 30 days of submission of the Final Report

- **Payment of Claim by Insurer:** If the Claim is not settled within the period of 30 days mentioned above, then the Insurer will pay Penal Interest of 2% above the rate applicable for a Savings Bank account.

Table 4: Claim Processing Timelines – General Insurance Claims

Particulars	TAT	TAT starts
Information by Insurer to Claimant of Detailed claim procedure	Immediately	Claim intimation
Appointment of Surveyor by Insurer	Within 72 Hours	Claim intimation
Submission of Survey Report by Surveyor to Insurer	Within 30 days	After appointment
Decision (acceptance/ rejection) on claim by Insurer	Within 30 days	After receipt of survey report
Claim payment by Insurer	Within 7 days	After accepting liability

CHAPTER 18
The Insurance Ecosystem

The Structure of the Insurance Market – Statutory,
Regulatory and Jurisdictional Relationships;
The Parliament and the making of Laws; The Regulator,
making Rules and Regulations, and Supervision of the Industry, the Ombudsman;
The Judiciary, providing legal protection and ensuring the delivery of equity to the
stakeholders, the Law Courts, Consumer Courts; Arbitration & Arbitrators;
The Market Players, Insurers, Agents, Brokers, Surveyors, TPAs

The Structure of the Insurance Market – Statutory, Regulatory and Jurisdictional Relationships

The Customer is the centrepiece, the core of the insurance market, its *raison d'etre*, the reason for its existence. That is stating the obvious. Let us get acquainted with the other important constituents of the insurance ecosystem. A diagrammatic presentation of the ecosystem is made through the medium of Figure 1.

The Parliament, that is to say the Lok Sabha and the Rajya Sabha, are perhaps the first, and the foremost components of this ecosystem for they make the laws which govern it. The laws mark out the boundaries of the market, of how the business will be conducted, of what is legal and legitimate. The Insurance Act, 1938 is the basic law governing the Indian Insurance market. While laws provide the foundation of the marketplace, the building blocks of the superstructure are the detailed rules and regulations, and these are provided by the market 'Regulator' appointed by Act of Parliament.

The Insurance Regulatory and Development Authority of India (IRDAI) is the 'Regulator' created by Parliament to act as the supervisor and market 'watch dog.' It is the Regulators primary function to formulate the detailed operational rules and procedures through which the laws will be implemented, and to supervise the day-to-day functioning of the marketplace. The IRDAI is presently headquartered at Hyderabad in the state of Telengana.

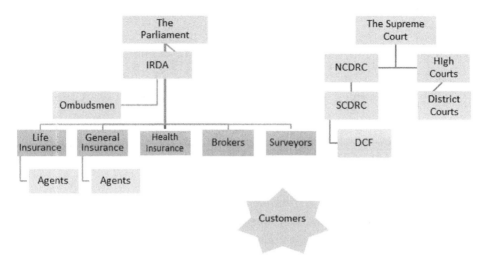

Figure 22: The Insurance Ecosystem

The IRDAI has issued a large number of comprehensive regulations governing the various areas of functioning of Life and General Insurance Companies, the Licencing and functioning of Intermediaries such as Agents and Brokers, the working of Insurance Surveyors, for the Protection of Policyholders Interests, in fact for every conceivable activity related to insurance business. It also conducts 'oversight' over the marketplace, playing the role of a 'Governing Body' and a 'Referee,' and it has the authority to punish and levy fines for breach of regulations by companies, intermediaries or surveyors.

Brokers function under Licence issued by IRDAI and distribute products for several Insurance Companies. They act as advisors to the buyer or Prospect, help him choose the most suitable product and during insurance transactions act as representatives of the buyer.

Agents, who also distribute insurance products, represent an insurance company. They have to obtain their professional licence from IRDAI and can only act on behalf of a single Insurer.

Surveyors too must obtain a Professional License to work from IRDAI. Their function is to act as independent entities for assessing the loss. They evaluate all the circumstances, evidence and records related to the event which has caused the loss, and quantify the amount of damage that has taken place. Their 'Report' on the causes and quantum of loss is the single most valuable input on the basis of which the Insurance Company takes a decision about whether the claim is payable and for what amount.

The **Third Party Administrator** or TPA, functions as an intermediary who delivers health claims management services on behalf of an Insurance Company to the claimants. Their functioning has been discussed at greater length in Chapter 10.

Complaints and Grievance Management: In spite of their best efforts, and the fact that a vast number of claims are paid out in quick time, it is impossible for an Insurance Company to fully satisfy every customer. At times some customers also have a genuine reason for dissatisfaction with the quality of service received by them, and the Insurance Companies have internal Grievance Management procedures, implemented as per regulatory guidelines, for reviewing customer complaints, many of which are then redressed in favour of the customer. However, some complaints remain unresolved. Let us say, there are always two sides to a story, and the final decision of the insurance company still does not satisfy the customer. The aggrieved customer has the option to now turn to 'The Ombudsman' for a solution.

The Ombudsman is a public 'Authority' created by a Government of India 'Notification' issued on 11th November 1998. He is appointed by the Insurance Council, the representative body of all Insurance Companies, on the recommendations of a special Committee consisting of Chairman IRDAI, and the Chairman LIC and GIC. The aim was to offer a quick mechanism from within the industry for solution of customer complaints without resorting to the regular judicial system. As such he is the representative of the Industry with two specific powers to (1) Conciliate disputes between Insurers and their aggrieved Customers (2) Make Awards. Though the Ombudsman therefore acts like a 'Court,' he is not a part of the judicial system. The procedure is simple. A customer can submit his complaint to the Ombudsman, free of charge, on a simple piece of paper. No lawyers are permitted to take part in the proceedings, and only the aggrieved customer directly or through an ordinary representative and the insurance company though its managers put up their respective points of view before the Ombudsman. The Ombudsman examines all the evidence and documents given to him and delivers his conclusion as an "Award' which is binding on the Insurance Company which cannot appeal against it, for the Ombudsman is regarded as an appointee and representative of the Industry which cannot appeal against itself. A customer who is not happy with the award can now seek justice either through the route of the 'Consumer Disputes Redressal' System, created under the provisions of Section 21 of the Consumer Protection Act, 1986, or the regular Law Courts.

The **Consumer Disputes Redressal System** consists of three tiers:

- **The District Consumer Form** (DCF) is the first level, located at almost every district. As on 31ˢᵗ August 2014, 629 District Forums were functioning at locations. The Insured can file his complaint before a DCF. All disputes involving valuation up to 20 lacs must be first made before the DCF. An appeal against the decision of the DCF, whether by the Insurer or the Insured, has to be made to the authority at the next level.

- **The State Consumer Disputes Redressal Commission** (SCDRC) is the next and appellate level. For complaints where value exceeds Rs.20.00 lac, but is less than Rs.1.00 crore, the case must be filed before the SCDRC. Presently there are 35 State Commission functioning.

- **The National Consumer Disputes Redressal Commission** (NCDRC) directly entertains complaints for values exceeding Rs.1.00 crore, and also hears appeals against the judgments of the State Commissions. It is located in New Delhi.

The Consumer Disputes Redressal system and procedure is simple, inexpensive and comparatively very fast, but the litigation is conducted mostly through professional lawyers, though a complainant can also present his own case.

The Supreme Court of India: An appeal against the Award of the NCDRC lies directly before the Supreme Court of India, and not before any of the High Courts.

The three tiers of this 'Consumer Disputes Redressal' system are considered 'quasi judicial' as they have limited, though lawful powers to decide consumer disputes under the provisions of the Consumer Protection Act, but do not have any judicial powers or role in the administration of justice. A customer may choose not to avail remedy under this system, and can prefer to proceed in the normal manner of filing a Civil Suit before the District Courts or High Courts.

This ecosystem has, by and large functioned, smoothly to ensure equity between the Insurer and Insured, though the speed with which it delivers results can be improved. Yet, the system functions in fine balance, and the various supervisory bodies such as IRDAI and the National Commission make sustained efforts to achieve a continuous improvement in its working.

Bibliography and References

(Endnotes)

1. Insurance; Retrieved on 20th February 2014; Wikipedia; http://en.wikipedia.org/wiki/Insurance.

2. Insurance Act, 1938; Sec 2(6B).

3. Ibid, Sec 64(VB).

4. The Principles of Insurance – Proximate Cause; Retrieved on 14th April 2014; http://www.cila.co.uk/files/Certificate/Chapter%208.pdf; The Chartered Institute of Loss Adjusters.

5. Indian Contract Act, Section 18 and 19.

6. Utmost Good Faith in Insurance Contracts; http://www.lawyersclubindia.com/articles/Utmost-Good-Faith-in-Insurance-Contracts-3098.asp#.U0561KKBk9M; Retrieved on 18th April 2014.

7. Uberrima fides ; From Wikipedia, the free encyclopedia; http://en.wikipedia.org/wiki/Uberrima_fides; Retrieved on 18th April 2014.

8. Kamal Nayan Kabra; 1986, Economic & Political Weekly, Nationalisation of Life Insurance in India ; Vol - XXI No. 47, November 22, 1986, http://www.epw.in/special-articles/nationalisation-life-insurance-india.html; Retrieved on 26th April 2014.

9. Katta Ashok Kumar et al; A REVIEW OF INSURANCE INDUSTRY IN INDIA; 2013; International Journal of Pharmaceutical Sciences and Business Management, Vol.1 Issue. 1, September- 2013, on pg 54 out of pg. 51–62.

10. History of insurance in India; Insurance Regulatory and Development Authority of India (IRDAI); Ref: IRDA/GEN/06/2007, Date: 12-07-2000; http://www.irda.gov.in/ADMINCMS/cms/NormalData_Layout.aspx?page=PageNo4&mid=2; Retrieved on 26th April 2014.

11. P S Palande, R S Shah, M L Lunawat; Insurance in India: Changing Policies and Emerging Opportunities; Sage Publications 203; page 49.

12. Ibid, pp 59–60.

13. Ibid, page 61.

14. First Annual Report, Insurance Regulatory and Development Authority of India, 2000–01, IRDAI, Table 9, International Comparison, page 21.

15. First Annual Report, Insurance Regulatory and Development Authority of India (IRDAI), 2000-01, IRDAI, Table 6, Key Market Indicators, page 17.

16. N.S. Vageesh and Mumbai Bureau; 25.11.2012; Private life insurers gain from forfeited balances of customers; The Hindu Business Line; http://www.thehindubusinessline.com/industry-and-economy/banking/private-life-insurers-gain-from-forfeited-balances-of-customers/article4133711.ece © The Hindu Business Line; Retrieved 06.06.2014.

17. Detariffication - Solutions News Letter; Marsh India Insurance Brokers Pvt. Ltd.; Extracted 25th July, 2014; [marsh.co.in/documents/Detariff.pdf].

18. Mayur Shetty; "Only 1 of 22 non-life insurers makes underwriting profits"; http://economictimes.indiatimes.com/wealth/insure/only-1-of-22-non-life-insurers-makes-underwriting-profits/articleshow/53854488.cms; 25 August, 2016, The Economic Times, Web Edition.

19. Annual Report, 2007-08, IRDAI; page 55.

20. The Insurance Act, 1938, Clauses 6(a), 6(b), 11.

21. C.K.Prahalad, The Fortune At The Bottom Of The Pyramid: Eradicating Poverty Through Profits; 2004; Wharton School Publishing.

22. Kashyap, Anthony and Krech; Microinsurance: Demand and Market Prospects – India; 2006; Federal Ministry for Economic Cooperation and Development, Germany; http://www.undp.org/content/dam/aplaws/publication/en/publications/capacity-development/microinsurance-demand-and-market-prospects-for-india/Microinsurance.pdf.

23. Health Insurance for the Poor; http://www.rsby.gov.in/about_rsby.aspx; extracted on 8th August, 2014; N.B. The section on the RSBY initiative has benefitted from the information provided on the website.

24. "German delegation visiting India to take Rashtriya Swasthya Bima Yojana lessons", The Economic Times. August 6, 2012, featured in the Wikipedia article "Rashtriya Swasthya Bima Yojana"; Wikipedia; http://en.wikipedia.org/wiki/Rashtriya_Swasthya_Bima_Yojana; extracted 8th August, 2014.

25. Lapsation of Life Insurance Policies, IRDAI, Annual Report 2007–08, page 25–26.

26. IRDAI (Protection of Policy Holders Interests Regulations), 2002, IRDAI, Clauses 3, 4, 6 and 7.

Bibliography

27. Save the Policyholder and Save the Insurer; Karnam Nagaraja Rao and Neha Chabraa, IRDAI Journal, June, 2014, IRDAI.

28. Claim Settlement in the Insurance Value Chain; P.C.James; IRDAI Journal, June 2014, IRDAI.

29. Protection of Policy Holders Interests Regulations; IRDAI; 2002.

Index

Abbreviations

Abbreviation	Expansion
BOP	Bottom-of-the-Pyramid, *a customer segment*
BPL	Below Poverty Line, *a customer segment associated most often with various Development Schemes administered by the Government*
BPP	Boiler and Pressure Plant Insurance
CAR	Contractors All Risks Insurance
CLI	Consequential Loss Insurance
CPM	Contractors Plant and Machinery Insurance
CRIG	Community Rural Insurance Group
D & O Liability	Directors and Officers Liability Policy
DCF	District Consumer Form
EAR	Erection All Risks Insurance
EEI	Electronic Equipment Insurance
FG	Fidelity Guarantee Insurance Policy
ICC	Institute Cargo Clause
IDV	Insured's Declared Value
IRDAI	Insurance Regulatory and Development Authority of India
ITC	Institute Time Clauses
ITC Hulls	Institute Time Clauses
MAR	Marine Policy
MB	Machinery Breakdown Insurance
MFI	Micro Finance Institution
NAIS	National Agriculture Insurance Scheme
NCB	No Claim Bonus
NCDRC	National Consumer Disputes Redressal Commission
P & I Club	Protection and Indemnity Club

P&I Cover	Protection and Indemnity Cover *for Ships, granted by P&I Clubs*
PA	Personal Accident
PMFBY	Pradhan Mantri Fasal Bima Yojna, *a crop insurance program of the Government*
PMSBY	Pradhan Mantri Suraksha Bima Yojna, *a Group Personal Accident Insurance Initiative launched by the Government*
PPD	Permanent Partial Disablement
PPHI	Protection of Policy Holders Interest, *Regulations issued by IRDAI in 2002 and 2017*
PSU	Public Sector Undertaking, *term used to refer to the 4 Government Owned Insurance Companies*
PTD	Permanent Total Disablement
RSBY	Rashtriya Swasthya Bima Yojna
SCDRC	State Consumer Disputes Redressal Commission
SFSP	Standard Fire and Special Perils Policy
SHG	Self-help Group
TAT	Turn Around Time, *a term used to indicate the assured time for completion of some task*
TPA	Third Party Administrator, *Third Party Administration*
TTD	Temporary Total Disablement
ULIP	Unit Linked Insurance Plan
WBCIS	Weather Based Crop Insurance Scheme
WC Policy	Workmen's Compensation Policy

Printed in Great Britain
by Amazon

80407678R00099